SECRETS I LEARNED BY SLEEPING WITH MY FINANCIAL ADVISOR

Personal Finance Habits, Strategy and Mindset

Alice von Simson

To Alex, thank you for sleeping with me.

To the six children we share; Violet, Willem, Emerson, Trinity, Jack and Baby P. Without you I would never have achieved the financial hardship that inspired me to write this. Thank you for helping me to become an author. I love you all!

Finally to Jane Mulkerrins, Tracy Blake, Olivia Walmsley and Tony Hazell, thank you for giving me my first chances to try my hand at newspaper writing. It was a gamble that I can't imagine paid off for any of you but I am eternally grateful.

SECRETS I LEARNED BY SLEEPING WITH MY FINANCIAL ADVISOR

Table of Contents

INTRODUCTION. LET'S TALK ABOUT MONEY, HONEY

This financial planning book is brought to you by Tinder! How is that for a unique selling point?

It all started in San Diego, California, when I swiped right on an accomplished and well-respected financial planner named Alex. Fortunately he had a thing for ditzy blondes with British accents so he returned the favor, and after I had run a background check and interviewed various neighbors and associates I agreed to meet him for coffee. I packed a police-grade mace gun in case he decided to get fresh and cross-examined him over a latte. What I discovered was mostly that I wanted him to take his shirt off, but we also discussed the fact that while I was very interested in the topic of personal finance, I had noticed that the same was not true for my peers.

"The information that you need in order to start saving for retirement is very simple," I told him, "but it feels overwhelming because most of the books and articles out there are written by financial experts who assume we already understand the basics. Also, they are often very boring."

His brow furrowed.

"I don't mean financial experts are boring!" I added, frantically backtracking. "I love financial experts; just some of the books are boring. If you wrote a book, it would be great! But you probably don't have time." Then, sensing a "subtle" way to trick him into seeing me again, I floated a brilliant idea.

"I could write a book," I suggested while mentally undoing the buttons on his pressed blue shirt. "And you could be the expert in it. I'm a journalist, so I know how to research a topic and simplify the information so that anyone can understand it. Books are a great source of passive income*," I added, throwing out a phrase I had heard on NPR. He looked mildly impressed.

The good news is that he asked me out on a second date, finally agreed to take his shirt off on date eight, and now we live together! The great news is that he also agreed to collaborate on the book. Obviously this means that there have been some compromises. For example, he made me promise not to use crude or sexual chapter headings such as "Financial Facts I Learned via Injection" because his clients are all very refined and probably don't want to hear about that sort of thing. However it has given me a unique insight into how the wealthy manage their money and provided me with a full-time fact-checker, researcher, and advisor. I'm not even kidding: we worked on this book in bed, in the car, on the beach, and at the kids' sporting events.

Now I want to share the secrets that I have learned by sleeping with a financial advisor with you. Unless you want to go out and find your own to sleep with, of course, in which case good luck to you.

If you have been putting off organizing your finances or speaking with a financial advisor because you feel as though you lack information, confidence, or both, then this book is for you. If you need help creating and building great financial habits that will serve you throughout a lifetime with minimal effort, you've come to the right place. I am not an economist or a financial expert and I won't be bamboozling you with annuities and futures in the first chapter. We will be talking about paying down debt, setting up an emergency fund, how to start saving for retirement, and how to get to the point where you can have a meaningful discussion with a financial advisor who can take care of the rest of it.

More importantly I will be teaching you to be your own coach so that you can remain open to and excited throughout the process. I will also be explaining the ways your brain will try to trick you out of achieving your financial goals and how you can get it back on track using information taken from scientific studies and real-life examples.

I've broken everything into simple steps that you can ultimately automate, and if you follow them you will be officially in control of your finances and, according to my bank manager, ahead of 98% of Americans in terms of financial preparedness. If that doesn't make you feel wonderfully superior, then I don't know what will!

You've already taken the first step toward optimizing your finances by picking up this book. If you are in a bookstore or on Amazon right now, then why not grab a folder to help keep you organized? I picked one that I like on my website ThisisYourBrainonMoney.com, which you are welcome to buy, but any folder will do. If you have one at home already, just use that.

Ready to whip your cash into shape? Let's do this!

*Passive income, in case you don't know, is money that keeps trickling in without you having to do much to maintain the flow. It is basically the best kind of money if you would rather spend all day watching reality TV instead of getting a real job. It is also the most elusive.

CHAPTER 1.
YOUR BRAIN
ON MONEY

One of my first writing jobs was for the financial pages of the Daily Mail in London. It was a celebrity interview segment called "Me and My Money," and in it I was allowed to grill the rich and famous about their relationships with their wallets. I asked them everything from how much was in their first paycheck to their worst ever purchase or investment. It was fascinating. These people—actors, musicians, military heroes—all had such different attitudes toward money. How they spent, saved, and invested it was colored by their life experiences, where they grew up, their parents' values, and in some cases by hard-learned lessons. Some were clearly well versed in the art of money management, while others turned a blind eye and hoped for the best.

It made me realize that while managing our money should be a simple exercise in mathematics it is clearly an extremely emotional topic. So while educating ourselves on the building blocks of personal finance is a great start, it is only one part of the picture. If we don't retrain our brains to support our new habits and to think logically and calmly around money, we are unlikely to meet our full potential.

Money is terrifying!

Brain scans have shown that we process not just financial loss but even the *idea* of financial loss in the amygdala, the same part of the brain that responds to mortal danger. That's why gambling can give us a rush similar to skydiving, and when we see horse number four trip over his own feet at the last fence we feel a lurch in our stomach and a prickle of sweat crackle involuntarily across our skin. Granted, the jockey, who is currently sailing over a pair of very expensive pointy ears, is probably experiencing something even more intense, but still it is there: a physical response to an impending financial loss that feels similar to a near-death experience.

We all process it differently, but for most of us it is unpleasant enough to be off-putting. For me it is an awful lurching sensation in my lady parts, as if I were riding in an elevator and out of nowhere it plummeted several floors, leaving my genitals in the penthouse and my body in the basement. It's no wonder managing our own money makes us nervous.

Money is also boring.

You would think that given the level of fear that financial mistakes create, your brain might respond well to something that could make you more competent around money, such as doing a little research to educate yourself. However, while our brains find financial *loss* terrifying, we find financial *education* very boring. Your brain accounts for 2-3% of your body weight but accounts for 20% of your metabolic and caloric expenditure (you really can think yourself thin!). It's a ruthlessly inefficient system, so our brains are always looking for ways to power down and think less. This is especially true when you try to make a decision that is complicated or emotionally laden, and financial decisions are both of these things. If you find yourself zoning out while listening to someone talk about finance, don't feel bad because most people do. In fact, studies have shown that when listening to financial experts talk, our brains respond by quietly shutting down the areas that control critical thinking and decision-making. Are you still with me?

In order to become successful money managers we need a new mindset.

Many of us put off organizing our finances because we don't feel confident enough to do so, but what if I told you that you don't need to be confident in order to succeed—you just need to be committed?

Like parenting there is no perfect solution for your financial situation. The only difference is that you cannot put off raising your children until you have figured out the ideal way to do it. Yes, there are a few tiger parents whose methods create Nobel Laureates in the family. For the most part, however, so long as your heart is in the right place and you make relatively sensible decisions you will end up with a productive member of society to brag about. If, on the other hand, you refuse to participate at all, you are guaranteed a feral, illiterate wildling who will show you up in public by biting people and pooping on the carpet. Think of your money as you do your kids (or your dog if you haven't got any). Refusing to participate in their care and growth isn't avoiding a decision; it is actively choosing neglect.

The great news is that successful money management can be boiled down to a few simple habits and by zoning in on these habits and overcoming the brain's objections to them, you will be able to change your life for the better. You will turbocharge your ability to build wealth, to pay down debt, and to see the bigger picture when you plan for retirement. This is crucial because when we allow our fear to prevent us from taking ownership of our money we lose that clarity, which is why most of us have so many questions about our own financial picture. Are we making enough money? Are we smart enough with our money? Have we made good enough choices with our money in the past? It can become so overwhelming that we shut down and become averse to even *thinking* about our money. We toss statements in the trash without reading them and lose track of what's coming in and going out of our homes. Want to know what most people with large amounts of debt have in common? They have no idea how much they actually owe.

Before we continue I would like you to reframe your perception of your money. It isn't the wild, untamable beast of your imagination; it's merely the family dog. It needs walking, feeding, and a little attention sometimes.

Ready to do this? Complete the following action steps and then meet me in the next chapter.

❋ ❋ ❋

A special note for my self-employed friends.

It can be very hard to create and stick to a budget or savings plan if you have a fluctuating income and no way of knowing what is coming in each month. I used this as an excuse to ignore my finances for years! Finally I decided to make a change and created a monthly wage for myself using my annual income for the past three years divided by 36 months. I backed off that figure a little to allow for a downturn and then set up a direct debit from my business checking into my personal account once a month for that amount. I skimmed any extra from the business checking into savings to be used for bad months or for unpredicted expenses. If I had a surplus at the end of the year, I slid it right into my retirement account. If you are in the same boat, then you too might benefit from creating an artificial salary using the above method before you proceed to the Action Steps.

ACTION STEPS

Today you are going to get some clarity on your financial situation so take a notepad or laptop, a fresh cup of coffee, and list the following:

ASSETS: Big ticket items that can be exchanged for cash. Examples could be a house, a car, a business, jewelry, or a particularly valuable baseball card collection.

SAVINGS: Retirement accounts, savings accounts, investment accounts, etc.

INCOME: What you have coming in each month from employment, child support, social security, ill-gotten gains, etc.

DEBTS: Mortgage, car payments, student loans, credit cards, etc.

EXPENSES: Bills, child support/alimony payments, rent, food, etc. Look at what you spent over the last 12 months to create an average for your monthly expenses.

We will use this sheet further on in the book, so keep it in your shiny new folder. Don't think of these numbers as good or bad; they are just the current numbers. You can change them later.

If you like you can download my free worksheet

from my website ThisisYourBrainonMoney.com.

Chapter Summary

- We process loss in the amygdala, which also processes mortal danger. This is why many of us are fearful around money.

- Our brains naturally power down when faced with complex or emotional decisions. Financial decisions are both.

- Most of us avoid clarity when it comes to our finances.

- We must change this mindset to become successful at managing our money. It's easier than you think!

CHAPTER 2.
HOW TO THINK
YOURSELF RICH

The first and most important step that I want you to take on this journey is to forgive yourself for the way you have handled your money in the past. Guilt is not a productive emotion. It stops you from moving forward and making impartial decisions for the future. How do we let go of guilt? Brooke Castillo, CEO and founder of the Life Coach School, discussed an interesting technique that she had come up with for over-drinkers on her podcast. I feel as though it could be helpful for many of us as we consider our past financial habits. She asks her clients to consider the part of their life that involved over-drinking as neither bad nor good but simply over.

Many of us have naturally applied this way of thinking to our memories of drinking in college. Was it responsible? No. Was it productive? No. Was it fun at the time? Yes siree! You've probably grown up and moved on to better things than binge drinking vodka Redbulls at 2 a.m., but you don't look back on that time of your life and feel guilty about it. It is simply over. So let's treat your financial history the same way. I'm sure you can actually conjure up some very positive memories that involved less than brilliant financial choices. That vacation you couldn't really afford? Those shoes? The year you ate out practically every night? It was a blast! But now you've moved on from that phase of your life and you have new goals. You will still have shoes and vacations and restaurant meals—don't worry. They just won't get in the way of the financial goals that are really important to you anymore.

I spoke briefly in the introduction about how our basic brain function is hampering our ability to succeed financially. Now I want to show you can turbocharge your thinking to achieve your wildest financial goals. I use the word *goals* instead of *dreams* here purposefully as dreams suggest an outcome that you are powerless over. Goals imply a more truthful narrative, which is that you are behind the steering wheel.

Become an exponential thinker.

Not enough time is spent discussing how the way that we think about money can affect our wealth. Two of Alex's most unlikely clients are an elderly couple: a teacher and a factory worker. I say unlikely because for the most part he deals only with people who have a high net worth (I am the exception!). We will call them Earl and Martha so that whenever I mention them, you remember that they are old. I am sorry if your name is Earl or Martha and you aren't old; I don't know what your parents were thinking. My middle name is Martha, which I find so humiliating that I lied about it on my visa application form and nearly didn't get to move to America! Anyway, back to our sweet elderly couple and how they accrued such a vast amount of money. It can be boiled down to two simple reasons: firstly they are old and secondly they are exponential thinkers and truly understand the power of investing.

The biggest handicap to becoming wealthy is the ease in which we humans engage in linear thinking and the difficulty that we have with exponential thinking. Up until a few hundred years ago, our lives were almost totally linear and were limited to the encounters that we had during our daily routines in the confines of a very small geographical area. Something happening on the other side of the world didn't just fail to affect us; we didn't even know that it had happened. In fact, we barely even understood that there was another side of the world. Here in the 21st century, something in Beijing cannot only affect us in New York but it can do so within minutes. Living in this exponential world creates an almost limitless space for growth so long as we can retrain our brains to think outside the box—or perhaps I should say: off the line.

If you put a dollar per day in your piggy bank for 30 days all of us can calculate that we will have $30 at the end of the month. That is a linear concept. It is simple, predictable, and something that we can all wrap our heads around. However, if we double the amount contained in our piggy bank every day, putting $2 in on the second day to make a total of $3, then putting $6 in the following day to make a total of $9, etc., after 30 days we would have $536,870,912. That is exponential growth, and the magnitude of the end result invariably comes as a shock to us.

We see the same rules at work when we look at charts of people who started investing in their retirements in their 20s versus their 30s. Those benefiting from an extra 10 years of compounding end up with a much larger pot, having invested considerably less of their own cash into it. Note that the person in the first example on the chart actually stopped contributing from the age of 45 and just let their money bring in a full-time wage all on its own.

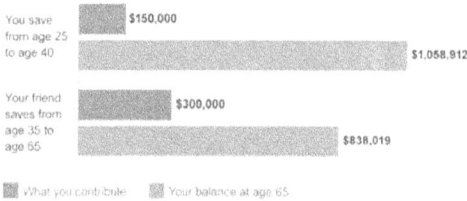

This table, published by Vanguard.com, assumes an annual 6% return. It doesn't account for inflation.

The opportunity cost of waiting to invest is so huge and so widely reported that it seems strange that people continue to hold off on getting started. However, the truth is that we simply find the difference that it would make hard to fathom. People are fascinated by Warren Buffet's wealth but a lot of it can be attributed simply to the fact that he invested in the stock market regularly and consistently for 75 years. This is something that we can all reap the benefits of whether we are a highly paid lawyer, a teacher, or a factory worker. The trick is simply to find our motivation as early as possible and to stick with it. When Earl explains the couple's wealth, he makes it sound so easy. "Every time we got a paycheck we used a portion of it to buy bonds. Every single check, since we were eighteen years old." Of course, the bonds of Earl's day paid considerably more than today's, but the lesson still stands. Investing consistently from an early age is key.

It's not what you earn, it's what you keep.

How much you earn from your job has a much smaller bearing on how much money you end up with later in life than you might think. We have all heard of the successful CEO who has gone bankrupt, seen the multimillion-dollar homes in foreclosure, and gloated over a once rich and famous celebrity working as a janitor 10 years after their star has faded. Equally, we have read the obituary of the unassuming secretary who lived in a cramped apartment but left $7 million in her will to a cat charity.

The difference between the cat lady and the CEO can be boiled down to their daily habits. Good financial habits, no matter how small, compound over time. In his book *Atomic Habits*, James Clear explains that "habits indicate your trajectory... and your net worth is a lagging measure of your financial habits. If you're a millionaire but you spend more than you make every month, then you're on a bad trajectory.... Conversely if you are broke but save a little each month you are slowly on the path to financial freedom.... Time magnifies the margin between success and failure. It will multiply whatever you feed it. Good habits make time your ally. Bad habits make time your enemy."

Wealth is invisible.

Their daily habits explain the conundrum of the secretary and the CEO perfectly, so why do we still find these stories so fascinating? Mostly it's the element of surprise. How can someone so *wealthy* end up in mountains of debt? And how did the wealth of the cat lady go *unnoticed* by friends, neighbors, and co-workers? We have great difficulty comprehending these two scenarios because we believe that wealth should be something that we can see. However, wealth in reality is almost completely invisible. It exists merely on the balance sheet or in the numbers at the bottom of a bank statement. When you see someone driving a Ferrari, you assume that they are wealthy when in fact all you can accurately surmise is that they have $175k less than they had before they bought the car. What we see when we look at fast cars, big houses, Rolex watches, and Chanel handbags are things, not wealth. The only thing we can safely assume about these people is that they *spend* a lot of money, but whether or not they *have* a lot of money is another story because spending by nature is the opposite of having.

You probably don't want to be a broke pop singer with a lot of watches, or a miserly old millionaire existing on canned soup. You want to be somewhere in the middle, and the trick to financial happiness is identifying your sweet spot and creating the habits that will support that trajectory. Today is a great time to consider your goals when it comes to having versus spending and some of the motivations and beliefs behind these compulsions.

Why are we so inconsistent?

Back to Alex's star clients, Earl and Martha. We now understand that these exponential thinkers created their wealth the same way that Warren Buffet did, with consistent investing. So what might hold us back from emulating this habit ourselves? The answer lies yet again in the human brain and its shifting priorities. In order to survive and thrive as a species we had to become adaptable. We see this reflected in our financial behavior as we travel through life. As children, our career ambitions are focused on enjoyment alone. We want to be farmers, dog trainers, or in my five-year-old daughter's case a contortionist. As we grow up many of us decide that these occupations aren't lucrative enough so we train to be nurses, lawyers, or realtors. Then we decide that these highly paid careers interfere with our desire to spend time with our children so we go part-time or became stay-at-home parents. When retirement comes along most of us will regret not making (or saving) enough money. We forget who we want to be in the long run and focus on who we want to be during each life stage, and our financial habits reflect that.

Only when we are older will we fully realize the benefits of all of the thousands of small contributions and sacrifices we have made. But if we want to be Earl and Martha, we need to think of our retirement contributions as non-negotiable, no matter what stage of life we are in, and understand that while the gains that we see now may be minimal, the very nature of compounding means that the greatest returns come toward the end of the process. A 4% annual return on your retirement account when you are in the early stages and have $10,000 saved up is $400, but by the time you reach $1m it will be $40,000. So if you do decide to become a stay-at-home parent, is your partner able to continue making these contributions for you? Equally, if you decide to quit your job to pursue a new passion, do you have enough savings to continue paying into your retirement plan while you transition? Sometimes the realization that we need to retire may even come at a time in our life when we are already over-stretched financially. In this case a complete overhaul of your financial picture may be needed. You may need to downsize everything from your rent to your bills in order to proceed, but it will be worth it.

Essentially, what I hope I've gotten across in this chapter is that you don't have to be a financial wiz to build wealth over your lifetime nor do you have to earn millions of dollars. All you need to do is tweak your financial habits as soon as possible and watch the benefits grow over time. As James Clear explains, a few degrees seems minimal when you look at it on a protractor, but set a flight path wrong by just a few degrees and you will end up in

Washington instead of New York. Setting yourself up for financial success doesn't necessary involve sweeping changes in your life—it may just be a few crucial tweaks here and there.

ACTION STEPS

1. Remember, being wealthy means different things to everyone and these values should define the way that you set up your finances.

2. Choose a few concepts that best represent your financial values and write them down. Examples could include Security, Freedom, Travel, Charity, Education, Time with Family, or Health, but yours may be different.

3. We will revisit your values and apply them to goals in the following chapter.

Chapter Summary

- Let go of unproductive guilt surrounding past financial decisions.

- Become an exponential thinker and acknowledge the power that the money you have today could hold in the future. The most valuable money is money that you invest while you are young.

- Remember, what you earn in life matters less than what you keep.

- Stay consistent and prioritize investing for retirement no matter what life stage you are in.

- Small habits create big changes.

CHAPTER 3.
HOW TO STICK
TO YOUR
VALUES

A t the end of the previous chapter you chose your financial values. Essentially what you want your money to do for you. They say that money can't buy happiness, but as my father used to say, money troubles can certainly cause unhappiness. Plus, although money may not be a magic ticket to nirvana and there are other factors that have a greater influence, such as health, a loving family, and so on, I do believe that if all other things are equal there are a lot of ways that money can and will buy you happiness. You love your kids, so how would it make you feel if you set up a savings plan and were able to help them pay for college or their weddings? Happy, am I right? What if you could contribute regularly to a charity that was close to your heart? Take a trip to Europe? Would that make you happy? Heck, I just treated myself to a manicure with a friend and guess what? That made me happy too! The trick to buying happiness is to learn how to make your money work hard for you. Once you have that down, you will find that motivation to stick to your financial goals is much easier to come by.

So in order to start buying yourself some happiness, first you need to figure out what sort of things really make you happy. If one of your financial values is family, then putting money into a college savings plan for your kids will make you happy. If one of your values is helping others, then budgeting for a regular charitable contribution will be very satisfying. If an important financial value for you is self-care, then a monthly massage or manicure will keep you feeling on top of the world.

Make sure your goals and your values align.

It is much harder to use your money as a tool to promote happiness when your financial goals and your financial values are out of alignment. For example, if your financial value is security but you are blowing all of your investible cash on a huge car payment and eating out four times a week, then you won't be as happy as you would if you had a fully stocked emergency fund and were making consistent contributions to a retirement account. Ensuring that the bulk of your money goes toward goals that align with your values will make you feel much wealthier without you having to go out and make (or spend) more money.

Let's go back to those values that you wrote down. Feel free to tweak them a little bit. Then pick the top 3-5 and list them in order of importance.

Once you have done this I would like you to think of some financial goals that complement your financial values. For example, if your value is travel then you might put "save for a trip to Europe." Having this value and this goal in alignment will enable you to feel at peace with all of the financial choices surrounding it and provides powerful motivation for sticking to your plans. For example, it is much easier to resist the buzz of buying a new butter-soft cashmere sweater from Nordstrom's when you know that same money can be put toward the far greater thrill of a picnic under the Eiffel Tower.

Become your own money mentor.

We will talk more about how to plan out and start saving for your goals further on in the book, but for right now I just want you to have some long-term visions for your finances. Then I want you to start thinking about becoming the type of person who you imagine easily attains those goals. This, according to James Clear, is a more effective way of changing your life than focusing on the goals and action steps that will help you to achieve them alone. I am currently testing it out and have found it to be extremely effective. Picture this: I am a single mom, who already has a business, five kids (we are a blended family; I didn't have to make them all from scratch, thank God), I am pregnant, and I am constantly being hit with demands on my time from other people: "We are looking for parent volunteers for the book fair on Friday." From my business: "I really should be reconciling this month's accounts." And from myself: "The house is an absolute mess. If someone comes over, they might call the cops. I better clean!"

I realized that I had been looking at writing a finance book as something *I would like to do*. With this in mind I was squeezing in a little writing or research at the end of the day when I was exhausted and only if I had finished everything else on my list. I was often struck with the realization that at this rate, writing this book would take me approximately three lifetimes and the likelihood of my completing it at all was approximately zero percent. My motivation had dropped to an all-time low.

Then I read *Atomic Habits* and tried adopting James Clear's mindset. I decided that I wasn't someone who wanted to write a book—*I was a writer*. And what kind of writer would try to cram their livelihood into 20 minutes right before bed-time? I started scheduling writing time during the day and regularly asked myself, "What would a writer do?"

A writer, I decided, would be consistent. They would write, even when they weren't really in the mood. They would have a dedicated writing space that was comfortable and clean. They would use their free time to do research, which I did by read-ing books in the bath and listening to podcasts in the school pickup line. Suddenly, I was making real progress. I moved from writing a few hundred words per day to a few thousand.

Think about how you can apply this technique to your finances. Want to become someone who is extremely financially responsible? What would Earl and Martha do? Would they set aside some time once a month to go over their financial goals? Would they prioritize paying down debt? Would they set up a retirement account and automate their contributions to ensure that they never missed a month? You bet they would. And this is you now. At the end of this chapter I am going to give you a bunch of action steps that are in line with your new persona of someone who actively manages their money. These are not just "things to do" anymore; they are the habits that define the new you!

Understand the cost of your choices.

Finally, once you have chosen your goals, you need to understand the cost of those choices, because nothing to do with money is ever free and all financial decisions come at a price, whether it is risk, tax, or sacrifice in another area. That cost might not just be financial; it could be emotional too, such as time away from family, creating discord with your spouse, or making do without some of the luxuries that you have become accustomed to.

Scott Adams once wrote: "One of the best pieces of advice I've ever heard goes something like this: If you want success, figure out the price, then pay it. It sounds trivial and obvious, but if you unpack the idea it has extraordinary power." If you already know what a decision will cost you and you make peace with that, it won't throw you off further down the road.

Create action steps for every goal.

Now that you have some solid financial goals written down and some powerful reasons to motivate you, we are going to take action. Look at your list again and write out an action or actions for each goal. For example if your value is security and your goal is to build an emergency fund, then an action item might be to set up a monthly direct debit into a savings account. You might have a secondary goal attached to that value, which is to contribute to a retirement account. In this case your action items might be to meet with a financial advisor and then set up a monthly contribution.

Separate and automate.

I am a huge believer in automating your money as much as possible. That way your savings take care of themselves and you can whip those contributions right out of your paycheck before you even see them. It's a fantastic and consistent habit that you can create without any work on your end.

I also like to keep my money separated into multiple accounts. For example, I have a checking account, a savings account where I keep my emergency fund, and the following investment accounts: a tax-advantaged retirement account, a regular retirement account, a college savings account for my daughter, a vacation account, and an account that I am using to save some money toward my daughter's first house deposit. The last goal aligns with my financial value of being able to spend time with family and my goal of never having my daughter stray more than one hundred feet from me. The money will be hers to put toward purchasing any house that is *near my house*! Don't judge.

I find that separating my money into different accounts helps me in terms of keeping organized and also because the temptation to borrow from an account that is specifically labeled for a goal is lessened. I can easily talk myself into putting a little something extra on my credit card or to impulse buy something using my current account, yet it feels irresponsible to spend money that is in my retirement account and immoral to spend money from my daughter's college account. Even siphoning money from the vacation fund feels like a sacrifice. Money that has a label and a plan is just harder to fritter away on shoes.

Before Alex dropped his pants and persuaded me to hand over all of my money for him to manage, I used Betterment, an online investing platform, or "Robo-Advisor" for most of these accounts. It allowed me to separate and label as many different "pots" as I wanted, and they offered different investment strategies based on my risk tolerance for each one. You can, for example, have your emergency fund set up as a regular savings account and your daughter's first house deposit fund (should you also be the controlling parent type) in an investment account with a more aggressive strategy given that she won't need it for the first 20 years or so of her life. There are several options out there if you are looking for something similar, including Wealthfront, Vanguard, and Ellevest, which is targeted at women and takes into account the facts that we often have a different lifetime earnings curve and a longer lifespan. Your financial institution may offer similar services and there will surely be new options once this book is published, so be sure to shop around and find the right fit for your circumstances.

Ramit Sethi, the author of *I Will Teach You How to Be Rich*, suggests keeping your savings in a completely separate institution from your checking account as it creates a better firewall between the two. It is less convenient and takes a little longer to borrow from your own savings, so he says you will be less likely to do it.

The important thing to ensure is that you can set up direct deposits into all of your accounts and that you can easily adjust them should the need arise.

Pay yourself first.

Direct deposits that come out of your account at the beginning of the month are without a doubt the most effective way to organize your money. They allow you to "pay yourself first," which means building savings into your budget rather than relying on money left over at the end of the month. Also, the automation allows you to set and forget the process, which requires less will-power and fewer organizational skills.

Businesses love setting up direct deposits from people's accounts because we swiftly get so used to the withdrawals that we no longer notice them and tend not to get around to cancelling them until long after we have stopped using the ser-vice. Think about how many gyms, subscriptions, and wine/book/cheese clubs you have joined and forgotten to cancel, wasting hundreds if not thou-sands of dollars. I want you to harness that power for your own savings. Figure out how much money you want to allocate from each paycheck toward your goals and send it automatically into a separate account. Then learn to live off what you have left over.

Your savings (particularly retirement) should al-ways be properly planned out and not just com-prise of whatever is "left over" at the end of the month. I use the same philosophy when I eat out at a restaurant. If I want to have leftovers for lunch the next day, I ask for a box at the beginning of my meal and separate my food into what I want to eat now and what I want to eat tomorrow. If I don't do that I have a tendency to nibble and pick beyond the point that I am full and wind up with a very meager portion for the next day. By putting "lunch" in a box first I am infinitely less tempted to borrow from it. It's still on the table, I can access it at any time, and yet psychologically there is a barrier.

As you get accustomed to this system, you can increase the amount that you dock from your own paycheck and challenge yourself to live off the remainder. If you are regularly broke by the end of the month, then you are probably already very good at this. We've all overspent at one time or another and spent the last week of the month turning down invitations only to spend the evening eating rice and beans on our couch with the light off. If your savings are truly dire, you may need to do this to yourself for a couple of months, but this time have your overspending be attributed to your own safety net fund, not shoes.

Start contributing now even if it isn't the full amount.

How much should you allocate to your savings goals? At this stage it is hard to say. For now I want you just to set up the accounts and start a direct debit for each of them even if it is only $20. This will get you used to your new system, get most of the hard work out of the way while you are motivated, and then you can gradually increase your contributions as you adjust your spending in other areas.

The best person to calculate a more accurate sum particularly for your retirement contributions will be a financial advisor as there are many factors to take into account: your income, your spouse's income, whether or not you own a house, when you plan to retire, how much and when you are likely to inherit. There is also the very personal question of how much you want to be able to spend when you retire versus how much you need to maintain an acceptable (to you) quality of life now. The trickiest question of all is when you plan to die. My point is that there is no magic number, convenient as that would be.

If you are not ready to sit down with a financial advisor or attempt these calculations yourself, then the following table may help to provide you with a very simplified version of the answer.

First you need to calculate your annual expenses (how much money you need each year to maintain your lifestyle). Assuming the 4% rule, which is that theoretically you could draw 4% of your principal every year and live on this indefinitely, you would need to save 25x your annual expenses to achieve financial independence. Write that figure down. The chart below will tell you how long that will take, depending on what percentage of your projected annual expenses you save each year. Decide in how many years you wish to retire and that will give you the percentage of expenses that you need to be saving each year. Divide that number by 12 for a monthly contribution.

For example, imagine I am a gorgeous, young 24-year-old (I can dream!) with no retirement savings and I want to have $100,000 per year to live off when I am 70. $100,000 x 25 = $2.5m so that is how much I need to have in my pot in 46 years' time (which is when I turn 70). The table says that if I have 46 years to invest I will need to put aside 15% of my $100,000 projected living expenses per year. This is $15,000, or if we divide by 12, $1,250 per month.

This is serious stuff so while this may give you a very basic starting point I cannot stress enough the importance of discussing your plans with an expert. Everyone's circumstances are different and a good financial planner will tell you where to prioritize in terms of paying off debt, saving for a house, and investing in retirement.

% of Annual Expenses Saved per Year	Time Required to Save 25x Annual Expenses
1%	100 Years
2%	86 Years
5%	67 Years
10%	54 Years
15%	46 Years
20%	41 Years
25%	37 Years
50%	26 Years
75%	21 Years
90%	19 Years

If you can't make this monthly contribution work then start with what you can afford now and then tweak the numbers as you go along. If your income is low and you are rolling your eyes (understandably) at this figure, then remember that Social Security should provide a sufficient degree of wage replacement. Just be sure to log into their website periodically to ensure that your contributions have been properly recorded. If you can afford not to rely on Social Security then that is certainly the safer option. The government assures us that it will still be around when we reach retirement age. Still it is better not to rely on others when it comes to something this important.

For the rest of your savings, just focus on choosing your goals and attaching a numerical value to them. So if one of your goals is to purchase a house, get online, find the type of house you want, figure out how much you can borrow and how much you need for a down payment. Divide that by the number of months you want to spend building those funds up and go from there. People who break their goals down into cold, hard numbers and then break those down into baby steps are much more likely to achieve them than those who don't and in much less time. Again, set up accounts and schedule a direct debit into them for as much as you can afford this month.

Now that you have locked sights on your goals and you know precisely what it is going to take to achieve them, give yourself a reminder so that on a daily basis you are forced to refocus on them. The home screen on your computer or phone is a great spot for this, as you will see it several times a day. Take a happy photo that reminds you of your goal and set it as wallpaper. This could be a photo of you holding a brochure for a vacation, a picture of you and your child in Disney ears, or a photo of you with a fistful of cash looking as elated as you plan to be when you have paid off all of your debts. Whenever you feel yourself wavering, take a moment to gaze at the picture and remind yourself of your path. It sounds silly but it really works! If you have kids, incorporate them into the picture. Those munchkins have a superhuman ability to guilt parents out of spending on themselves, so we may as well harness it in a way that benefits us in the long run.

ACTION STEPS

1. Set financial goals, then open individual, labeled accounts for them. Find an institution that won't charge separate fees for all of your "pots." Online institutions tend to offer better interest rates on savings than brick and mortar ones. Try Alliant High-Rate Savings, Ally, or Barclays Online.

2. Automate your contributions even if it isn't the full amount yet. You can adjust that later.

Chapter Summary

- Figure out your financial values; i.e., how money can make you happy.

- Choose goals that align with those values.

- Start to see yourself as someone who is good with their money, and the habits to support this will follow.

- Acknowledge that all decisions come at a cost and make peace with that.

- Capitalize on automation to pay yourself first and reap the benefits of the "set and forget" method.

- If you can't contribute the full amount to a goal, start where you can. Creating the habit is important.

CHAPTER 4
WHY YOU
SHOULD KEEP
YOUR MONEY

B efore I started my research for this book, I assumed like many that if I wanted spare change to put toward my retirement I needed to earn more money. The internet is brimming with ideas for side hustles ranging from second jobs to earning $10 per day filling out surveys. However, actually keeping the money you already have makes a difference to your finances much faster than bringing home more bacon. Why? Because of the IRS. All of us have a personal allowance, which is money that we are allowed to keep tax-free. Anything that we earn beyond that is taxable at an increasing rate. So if you made $50,000 as a single person in 2019, your standard deduction (of approximately $12,200) is tax free. You pay 10% on the following $9,700 and 12% until you reach $39,475. From there you pay 22% until you reach $84,200. This means that if you save $10 then you get to keep the whole $10. If you earn an extra $10, you only get to keep $7.80. Essentially, the more money you make, the less you get to keep, so although of course making more money is still a good idea, a great way to boost your retirement or savings account is simply to keep more of the money that you already earn.

In addition to this, money that you save *today* is more powerful than any money that you can make in the future. This is because if invested wisely, its value will increase over time. So $1,000 invested now will almost always be more valuable than $1,000 earned in 10 years' time. In fact, saving consistently over your lifetime is so important that the government offers all kinds of tax incentives to do so because, selfishly, they want you to pay for your own diaper changes at the Senior Living Center.

Not saving is expensive.

The rewards of investing early and consistently are clear, but it is worth adding that the decision *not to save* tends to come at a very high cost. Financial institutions have exploited our naturally poor ability to manage money by creating what is called an "artificial bottom" (nothing to do with Kim Kardashian). In previous generations, when we had spent all of our money, we could no longer buy anything. Now thanks to them, we have easy access to overdrafts and credit cards. These institutions then penalize us harshly for small mistakes, raking in for example $34 billion in overdraft fees in 2017 alone, according to a Market Watch report from Moebs. It is likely that those paying the biggest proportion of those fees are the 29% of American households with less than $1,000 in savings, for whom a single emergency can spell disaster (Federal Reserve, FDIC, and MagnifyMoney estimates, June 2019). Commit to yourself that the next time your car breaks down on the road, the biggest inconvenience will be waiting for the tow truck, not figuring out how on earth to pay rent and fix your car at the same time.

Why you hate saving.

Clearly the economic reasons for saving are compelling, so why aren't we doing it? Ted Klontz, a financial psychologist and professor at Creighton University, suggests that it is a hangover from our tribal past. Until very recently humans lived communally. Keeping something that you didn't need was considered selfish, and such behavior could have you kicked out of the group. You also had several generations under one roof all providing for each other, and a shorter life expectancy meant that even the concept of saving up for several decades of not working would have been incomprehensible.

Another reason that we have little desire as a species to save is that for thousands of years we have been reliant on frequent hunting trips for survival. A bad hunt could mean death, which gives us plenty of instinct to go out into the workforce, but without the means to preserve food, we learned to place very little value on keeping anything "extra." Since then our lifestyles have changed at such a pace that our brains have been unable to keep up. We only have a thin crust of cells and neural circuits standing between us and the brain of a caveman, which means that until our heads receive a much needed update from the app store we won't benefit from any inbuilt instincts to stock our savings accounts. Or at least not in the same way that we have instincts to find a mate, reproduce, or provide for our families in the short term. Having said this, some people do seem to be naturally better at saving than others, and this is worth exploring to see if we can retrain our brains to get on that train.

Why you think you can't afford to save.

The reason that most Americans give for not saving is that they can't afford to do so. The reality is that this is because they consider savings to be what you do with *leftover* money, rather than something to prioritize. If you look at people in third world countries who live in miserable poverty surviving on $2 per day, you will find that most still set aside something for the future.

Scientists have tried to explore why it is that some countries are so much better at saving than others. One rather fascinating hypothesis has to do with the way we speak, as one of the common denominators between countries with good savers has been "futureless" language, where the grammar doesn't make a clear distinction between the present and the future. They argue that this may create less of a psychological barrier to the process of denying oneself now in order to benefit further down the road.

My suspicion is that it is in fact our comfortable first world life giving us a false sense of optimism that our financial circumstances will invariably get better. Most people who "can't afford to save now" believe that they will be able to in the future. Although in reality what usually happens is that even if we do end up earning more, our spending increases perfectly in line with it, whereas our savings do not. The various safety nets that we have set up as a society also mean that much of the urgency of providing for our families in a crisis has been alleviated. There are free medical clinics, food stamps, and shelters if things get really tough. It's not ideal but it's not death either.

Why you (and I) just love to spend!

To make matters worse, we Americans (and British ex-pats) have compounded a lack of fear of running out of money with a societal bias toward relentless consuming. We all now live well above our means with easy access to borrowing and seductive incentives to do so. Thousand-dollar iPhones are seen as necessities and vast jumbo-sized flat screen TVs the norm, and all large purchases come with the offer of a payment plan. In fact, when you purchase a car these days, the salesman is likely to tell you the monthly payment that you will make on a new vehicle while glossing over the actual purchase price. For us Millennials in particular the system of purchasing items on credit is so ingrained that saving up for something feels oddly old-fashioned.

We have become very expensive to maintain.

My editor asked me a very interesting question as he worked on this chapter. Younger people, he said, have become minimalists, with much less stuff in their homes. Does this mean they are buying less, though, or just different things? It brought to mind an article that I read a couple of years ago on spending habits. Rather than conspicuous consumption (think Ferraris, Luis Vuitton purses, and red-bottomed shoes), the wealthy are now engaged in "conscious consumption"," which from the outside does indeed look like minimalism. Think free-range, macrobiotic superfoods, electric cars, organic cotton, yoga retreats, therapy, and so forth. The new trend for aspirational millennials is not to spend on things but to spend on oneself.

Not that this spending is completely invisible, of course. California is full of young, blonde, tan, busty women, but how many of them are in fact Botox-ed brunettes with a spray tan and fake boobs? I've got to hold my hands up here and admit that I am merely two bags of silicone short of belonging in this demographic (although obviously in public I claim coconut oil and an invented Swedish grandmother).

Clearly we should all be exploring our reasons for

any overspending on our personal appearance as well as looking for ways to save. A lot of these compulsions, however, must have to do with environment and the competition to attract a mate. Young American men, raised on a diet of extreme prudishness over public nudity and hardcore porn, more or less expect fake breasts. European men, who have been subjected to a childhood of nude beaches and public changing rooms, think they have scored if you can't tuck your nipples into your socks. Similarly, if all of your friends get Botox then it isn't much fun being the only one who looks conspicuously older. While spending on these procedures could have been considered symptoms of a self-esteem issue when they were first introduced, we have now become so used to them that for many women they feel no different to getting their ears pierced or spending money on clothes. But in the same way that we can reduce or at least save money on eating out, there are ways to save on these expenditures. Can you get some of your beauty treatments on Groupon or Living Social? Does your local beauty school offer highlights for a more affordable price than the salon? Or can you find a cosmetologist, masseuse, or nail person who is willing to trade for a skill that you possess? I offer this advice not just for women as nowadays men too are getting Botox, pedicures, and more expensive haircuts.

Now that two breadwinners have become the

norm at home, the other invisible luxury that we like to blow our paycheck on is time. We pay cleaners to pick up after us, and according to the US Department of Agriculture we now spend more than half of our food budget on eating out (as opposed to one-third 50 years ago). I am not here to lambast you for that. A cleaner whom you pay $15 per hour is a sensible investment for a professional who works long hours bringing in far more than that.

At the end of the day, time is the one thing that you can't get back. In fact, several budgeting experts have suggested weighing the merits of certain purchases against *how long* it would take you to earn them. For example a $100 meal for two might cost an attorney 15 minutes but it would cost someone making $10 per hour 10 hours. I would suggest doing the reverse of this when it comes to making decisions about outsourcing tasks. If subscribing to a meal delivery service saves you five hours a week in shopping, prepping, and cooking time then is the additional cost worth it to you? As a self-employed person this is even more important to ponder because you may be purchasing back time that you could use to earn more money.

Spending on education has also increased, particularly for women and especially for those of us who have to distract men from our lack of fake boobs with scintillating conversation! I'm only joking of course; I have a padded bra for that. It isn't just the fact that we are becoming more educated as a nation, but that the cost of that education has increased eight times faster than wages, according to Forbes.com. This alone could easily account for the dire state of young people's savings accounts.

Finally we have made it much too easy to spend. You can literally buy a new grill on Amazon using your phone while waiting at a stoplight. Or a $400 blender or a 15-foot artificial Christmas tree that is too tall for your ceiling but too expensive to pay the return shipping on. Nobody is perfect, least of all me. We will discuss this further in the habits chapter, but if you are serious about saving money then unlinking your credit cards from online stores will at the very least cause enough of an inconvenience to make you pause before purchasing unnecessary items.

Saving isn't sexy.

While the banks will actively seduce you into borrowing, not so hot are their incentives to save. Regular savings accounts currently offer rates well below inflation, which is off-putting to consumers to say the least. Studies have shown that people are unlikely to deny themselves in the present if they don't feel there is "sufficient compensation" in the future. That is, they might save $1,000 for a year in exchange for $1,200 at the end but are unlikely to do so in exchange for $1002. The only way to get better returns on your savings is to take on an investment strategy with more risk, but as we have discussed, our fear-driven amygdalas often try to talk us out of that even if the risk is low and the long-term outcome likely very positive.

In order to succeed, you must become acquainted with your future self.

In researching this topic I found that I could relate in some way to all of the above reasons, or rather *rationalizations*, for not saving. The next one, however, hit home the most and in fact reminded me strongly of my childhood.

When we were kids, my sister was a natural saver while I was a natural spendthrift. Her urge to hoard led her to exhibit strange behaviors such as lining up her Easter chocolate on the shelf above her bed and refusing to touch it (or let me touch it) for months. It would drive me into a state of slobbering anxiety. I would beg and plead and throw myself at her feet, but she showed no mercy. Then, after the chocolate had dried out and developed a white crusty shell, she would casually offer to give it to me in exchange for some favor or toy, then watch with a look of disgust as I wolfed it down.

If ever there were a poster child for failing the marshmallow test, it would have been me. If you are unfamiliar with this experiment, it involved taking individual children and seating them at a table with a single marshmallow in front of them. It was explained that they could choose to eat the marshmallow immediately or save it for a designated amount of time and receive two marshmallows in return for their patience. The researchers followed the children's progress throughout their lives, and it was revealed that the kids who were able to exercise self-control to reap the bigger reward were more successful all the way through to adulthood. Although the study didn't go into specifics, it is likely that these children would also have turned out to be better savers as they were less impulsive and clearly had an easier time identifying with their future selves than those who failed the test. If you strongly feel as though you are saving money (or marshmallows) for your own benefit, then it is much easier to stay motivated. If you have a hard time picturing yourself in the future, as I always have, then the same savings can feel as though you are denying yourself for the benefit of a stranger.

Learn how to train your naughty subconscious.

In summary we have five excuses that our brain makes to try to trick us out of saving.

1. Due to our tribal past we have no real instinct to do so.
2. We believe savings should consist of "leftover money."
3. We feel no urgency to save, as we aren't likely to starve or be denied emergency medical care for lack of funds.
4. There appears to be little compensation for saving in the linear sense.
5. We have a hard time identifying with our future selves.

How can you circumnavigate these obstacles to become a super saver?

The key is to learn how to speak to your subconscious. Ninety percent of our decisions are made by it so we must learn to speak its language. The subconscious does not respond to graphs and charts; it responds to pleasure and fear, so we must learn to portray our savings goals in this manner.

The "Disturb" is a technique financial consultants use that involves presenting the client with a dire vision of their future. Doing this to yourself should stimulate you to take action, as suddenly saving becomes the least painful rather than the most painful option. With the costs of health-care and accommodation in old age uncertain, we ought to be squirreling away a good chunk of our annual income. Trust me, if you thought having children was expensive then try raising an old person.

Picture the last years of your life. Where are you? What does it feel and smell like? Are you wearing the scratchy off-brand adult diapers or the cushy Depends? Do you want your annual treat to be an Alaskan cruise with the grandkids or a trip to the local diner for the early bird special? Which, by the way will be served to you through a straw via a blender if you can't afford teeth. Try to involve as many senses as you can to visualize this.

Brad Klontz, a financial psychologist, also suggests using an aging app to create a picture of your future self, . He claims that when you show a 30- or 40-year-old person a photo of themselves at 80 or 90, their savings rate increases dramatically, up to 200%, presumably because it makes you realize that aging is not a vague concept but a definite reality. Try this yourself. Suddenly you may find that living within your means will no longer consist of simply staying in the black through to the end of the month but will also include providing for your future (adorable) old-person self.

Now that you have thoroughly frightened your

subconscious, it is time to offer it some pleasure. You can do this by regularly picturing the fruits of your savings goals. Involve as many of your senses as you can and try to enjoy the journey to the goal as much as possible. If, for example, you are saving for a trip to Paris, then start listening to French music, eating French food, sketching the Eiffel Tower, and learning French. By living the experience of your goal in the present, you will naturally be motivated to contribute to it in the present.

ACTION STEPS

Now that we have created some fear and some urgency, it is time to capitalize on it by looking over our finances with a view to making retirement and savings a priority no matter your life stage or circumstance.

1. Deduct however much you need to save from your monthly paycheck and assign the "leftover money" to everything else. Use the table from Chapter 3 to figure out a reasonable number for your retirement contribution if you have yet to meet with an advisor.

2. Set up an automatic debit from your checking to your savings or retirement account at the beginning of each month for an amount that is as close to the previous number as you can get it.

3. If possible, set up savings accounts labeled with specific goals. This creates a bit of a firewall between you and that money and it should give you some extra motivation to nurture its growth when you see that it is destined for a specific purpose.

Chapter Summary

- Due to taxation, saving more is more effective than earning more,

- Money that you invest today is more powerful than money you make in the future.

- Choosing not to save can be costly.

- You have no natural instinct to save so you must retrain your subconscious.

- You must prioritize your savings and see them as non-negotiable, like rent.

- You must become friends with your future self.

CHAPTER 5
HOW TO CREATE FABULOUS FINANCIAL HABITS

I spoke briefly about the importance of fostering great financial habits in the Introduction. This truly is the secret sauce of financial success, determining whether time will be your friend or your enemy when it comes to your money. While I don't agree that you should forgo all earthly pleasures, switch lattes for puddle water, and start making your own yogurt, it is true that the very smallest of steps can have a great impact. If you improve enough aspects of your financial picture by as little as 1%, that will be enough to have a big impact over time, particularly if you keep adding and fine-tuning along the way. Rome wasn't built in a day as they say, but if you work regularly and consistently, over time you too can build a very attractive financial future.

Good habits are hard to make. bad habits are hard to break.

It sounds simple and painless to tweak a few small habits and I am sure you are feeling as though it all should be rather easy. I am glad that you feel this way, and I want you to know that I believe in you too! I know that you can do this, but before we jump right in, I just want to make you aware of some of the tricks that your brain may use to talk you out of these actions and what you can do to outsmart it.

Charles Duhigg, the author of *The Power of Habit*, and an expert on behavioral psychology, suggests that most people fail to adopt new habits because they do not understand the structure of them. All habits, good or bad, follow the same pattern.

1.) Trigger or cue. This is what makes you perform the habit. Boredom might make you browse on eBay; tension might make bring your fingernails to your lips; sitting at your desk first thing might make you think of coffee.

2.) Action. This is the action part of the habit loop. It's where you start mindlessly shopping or nibbling your nails or it's where you might get up to pour a coffee.

3.) Reward. This is where your brain receives the reward for performing the habit. The buyer's rush, the relaxation from nibbling your nails, the caffeine hit from the coffee.

Most bad habits have obvious and immediate rewards, but good ones such as going to the gym or contributing to a savings account often take time to have a beneficial effect on the brain. Thus, bad habits become ingrained very easily while good habits are much harder to instill. Finance has become a huge passion of mine, and still I get much giddier when I impulse-buy a sweater than I do if I tuck a little extra into my retirement fund. The trick, Charles Duhigg says, is to create your own reward system.

When I sit down to go over my monthly budget, I make it as luxurious of an experience as I can. I fix myself a fancy hot drink, or grab a dark chocolate sea salt bar, set myself up at my desk, and bask in the sugar rush while I do something that I would otherwise find very dull. It means that my brain doesn't automatically go into full horror mode when I get a calendar reminder to perform this task. Is there something that you could reward yourself with for the good work that you are doing *right now* by reading this book? Maybe a leftover brownie? A glass of wine? A cigarette? Okay, maybe not the cigarette. That's bad for your health and your money. How about a little square of dark chocolate?

The other problem that we face is simply forgetting new habits before they have time to take hold. Think of the habits that you do without fail and without much thought every day: brushing your teeth, drinking coffee, locking the front door. These are so ingrained that your brain is basically on screensaver as you are doing them. When you try to add a new habit, such as weighing yourself, it can easily be forgotten after a few days because performing it requires independent thought.

The final reason why people often fail to stick to new habits is because they might be unrealistic. Tiny habits are very easy to start and stick with and you can easily build on them. Instead of going on a draconian financial overhaul where you never have a latte again and eat nothing but rice and beans, how about you commit to changing your route to work so you don't pass the café that tempts you? Perhaps avoiding that cue will be enough for you to drop the habit at least on a daily basis without you even noticing. Or what if you were to start a direct deposit into your savings account of just $100 a month and gradually increase it over time? If you want to retire in any sort of luxury you ought to be saving a lot more than that, but if you are nowhere close to that number now now, how about starting with 5% of your paycheck and increasing this by 1% every few months?

While good habits can be hard to entrench into our lifestyles, bad habits are the opposite. They are almost never forgotten, and often the cues and actions are so deeply ingrained that they can re-surface years after a habit has been dropped. Just ask any smoker.

So how do we go about dropping our old, naughty habits and picking up new, good ones?

Establish your "why."

Brooke Castillo, whom I quoted earlier, says that people who desire to change old behaviors and create new ones have a better chance of succeed-ing when they have a compelling "why" or reason to do so. This makes perfect sense, so before we start planning, why not think about your reasons for wanting to change your financial behavior? What was it that drove you to pick up this book in the first place? Think about your "why," write it down on a PostIt note, and stick it on your bath-room mirror. Focus on it for a couple of minutes twice a day while you brush your teeth. You can also add it to any calendar reminders that you decide to set yourself for financial tasks.

Then let's start planning for success. Take a sheet of paper or download my financial habits worksheet from www.thisisyourbrainonmoney.com and write down all of your good financial habits. Then on the other side, write down the bad ones. Good habits might include making your own coffee, contributing to your company's 401k, paying your bills on time, etc. Bad habits might include poor meal planning that results in food waste, overspending on entertainment, etc. Don't criticize yourself as you do this; instead try to look at your list as a scientist might, with total detachment. Next I want you to think of some new good habits that you would like to introduce into your routines: making your own lunch, for example, or planning your monthly spending and taking five minutes per day to check your progress.

Stack one good habit onto another.

First let's work on integrating the helpful, new habits into your life. Looking again at the structure of habits, we have:

1. Trigger or Cue
2. Action
3. Reward

In *Atomic Habits*, James Clear suggests a technique to smoothly integrate new habits into your routine by piggybacking them onto an old one. The end of the old habit creates a natural cue for the new one. For example, if you want to weigh yourself every day then do it right after an already ingrained daily habit, such as brushing your teeth. You may need a reminder at first but soon the action of rinsing your toothbrush and replacing it in the mug will automatically trigger you to step onto the scale. If you log in to your bank account once a month to check that your paycheck has been deposited, why not make a habit of adding a little extra to your savings account at the same time? When you deposit your tax return check, can you see this as a trigger to squirrel away a percentage into your retirement fund? When you make your morning cup of coffee, can you pour a second serving into a to-go cup so that it's ready for you to grab as you walk out the door and you aren't tempted by the café on the way to work?

Specify the time, manner, and place of new habits.

The other key, according to Clear, is to specify the time, location, and manner in which you will perform a task. Stating that you will create a monthly budget is too vague. Get specific here and plan out the details before you schedule it into your calendar. For example, "I will sit down at 9 a.m. on payday at my desk and spend 15 minutes on my budget, while eating a muffin." I threw in the muffin part as a reward for compliance. It will make your brain associate this task with pleasure and you will be less likely to put it off when the day arrives. We are all golden retrievers at heart.

Finally, for tasks that occur infrequently, basically anything that isn't a daily habit, I like to make the final part of performing the task scheduling the next occurrence. For example, when I go to the gym, before I leave the building I look at my calendar, decide what day and time I am going to come in next, and I put that into my calendar. If I don't do this then weeks or even months could pass before I find myself back there. No matter how long I have been working out, I literally never wake up with a natural urge to do it.

Change your environment to nix your bad habits.

Next we need to tackle those naughty habits. Have you ever noticed how some people seem to have great willpower while others really struggle? Scientists tried to examine how those in the first group were able to demonstrate such temperance only to discover that there was actually very little difference in the levels of willpower between the two groups. It turned out that the first group of people had simply discovered a very effective technique to eradicate bad habits and that was removing all of the cues from their environment. If they wanted to lose weight, for example, they didn't merely resist the urge to eat junk food. Instead they removed all of the junk food from their house and avoided those areas in the grocery store entirely.

Redesigning your environment to reduce negative cues and encourage positive ones is a surefire way to promote success. Take a moment to think how you might take advantage of this. Could you take a new route to and from work to avoid locations that promote impulse spending? Could you order your groceries online to avoid the temptation of impulse purchases? Could you remove loose cash from your wallet and keep it in a safe place in the home instead? If the triggers aren't there then the need for willpower is lessened considerably.

Make bad habits less appealing.

Now that we have removed as many cues as possible, it is time to make the action step of the habit loop harder to take. It is easy to snack on candy that is in your desk drawer. Would you want it as much if you had to walk to the kitchen, fetch a stool, and take it down from the top shelf? Would you make that little impulse purchase on Amazon if you had deleted your saved credit cards and had to enter the numbers manually? Would you spend cash as easily if you had to drive home to get it? By creating your own barriers to bad financial habits, you can make them much less appealing.

Start s***ting in your own cereal.

The final step is ruining your own reward. This sounds mean but it has to be done. Once you brain has experienced a crappy version of a reward a few times, it will start to lose interest in performing a habit. How can you make bad financial habits less rewarding? Sometimes just verbalizing what you are doing can take the shine off. For example, try saying out loud, "I am wasting money online that I should be putting into our savings. This is hurting my family's finances," next time the urge to browse Amazon hits. It might be enough to help you to resist. Other people try snapping a rubber band against their wrist to create an association between the bad habit and physical discomfort. If you want to go back to your golden retriever alter ego, then maybe try smacking yourself in the nose with a rolled-up newspaper whenever you make a bad purchase. The funny looks you would receive in public might be even more motivating!

Spend time nurturing your new habits.

Now that you have identified your positive and negative financial habits, spend the next few days really focusing on them and fine-tuning the steps that you need to take to get them fully ingrained in your psyche. Remember you are now someone who actively manages their money and act accordingly. Once you feel confident that these habits are here to stay, use them as a springboard for even better habits. For example, once you have got used to putting 10% of your paycheck into savings, see if you can raise it to 11%

ACTION STEPS

Identify your good and bad financial habits and make a list.

Try to adopt the following positive habits as well as those you have chosen for yourself.

1. Automate your savings so the money is whisked straight from your paycheck and into your savings account. You won't miss what you don't see.
2. Read at least one finance book per year. This will keep you motivated and in-formed, and you are likely to gain tips that will help you optimize your financial habits.
3. Change the Joneses that you keep up with. Keeping up with profligate people does you no good. Follow a few thrifty in-fluencers and shrewd investors on social media for inspiration.
4. Commit to making small but meaningful changes in your spending. Increase your savings rate by 5%, cut your spending on entertainment by 10%, cancel a sub-scription service that you rarely use, pay your bills early.
5. Drive your car for an extra few years after

it's paid off and put what you were used to spending on a car payment into your retirement fund. Do the same for any other loans that you have paid off. You won't miss that money as it was already leaving your account every month.

6. Examine your spending each month and look for areas that you could improve upon.

7. Learn to say no to your kids. They are developing their own spending habits based on what they see. If they are used to having something purchased for them every time they leave the house, this is what they will do with their own money later. It is never too early to teach good financial habits. Teach them to bring a water bottle and a snack when they leave the house and limit impulse buys.

8. Revisit your goals often and visualize them using all of your senses. Do something every day that reminds you of them or change the wallpaper on your phone to reflect them.

9. Set monetary goals when it comes to paying off debt or adding to your savings and give yourself a reward when you reach them.

10. Keep yourself informed. Commit to opening bank and credit card statements as soon as they arrive. Read through them

to check for fraud or subscriptions that you forgot to cancel and keep an eye on how much interest you are paying.

Chapter Summary

- Creating good, consistent financial habits is the secret to financial success.

- Good habits are hard to make; bad habits are hard to break.

- Mimic the "instant gratification" reward pattern of bad habits for your good habits; for example, giving yourself a square of chocolate for writing out your monthly budget.

- Try to ruin your rewards for bad financial behaviors.

- Identify your "why" or reason for changing your financial behavior and keep it at the forefront of your mind.

- Stack good habits together.

- Get specific when you plan out a good habit. Decide on the time, manner, and place.

- Change your environment to remove cues for bad habits and place cues for good habits.

CHAPTER 6 HOW TO OPTIMIZE YOUR DEBTS AND THEN PAY THEM DOWN

Between mortgage, credit cards, and student loans, most of us have some level of debt. One way to increase the amount of money that we can contribute toward the financial goals that bring us joy is to claw back some of the money that we are spending on interest each month. I want you to get excited about this. No, really! Closely examining our debt is scary and unpleasant; however, interest paid on debt is one place where you can save money without making any sacrifice in terms of lifestyle. Cutting out Starbucks might save you $5 per day but the cost is missing out on a treat. Cutting the interest on your borrowings by refinancing or consolidating saves you money without you having to change a thing about your daily routine. That money can go straight from the banker's golf club fund to your Paris fund or retirement. It's your money, damn it. Take it back!

Take a deep breath and a good look at your debts.

We are ultimately going to want to pay down some debt and we will formulate a plan for that later. But for now I just want you to lay out all of your debts and all of the interest rates and then see how we can optimize them so that you start paying less interest *this month*.

Print out or open your latest credit card or loan statements and list everything you owe, the interest rates on each loan, and the terms (how long that rate applies and how long you have to pay it back). Once you have them all listed, try to arrange them in order of the nastiest debts (those with the highest interest rates) down to those with the lowest interest rates and those with tax-deductible interest (mortgages, student loans). We aren't going to worry too much about the latter. This chapter is for clearing toxic debt only. For most people the costliest debts are on credit cards. For some people, payday loans, gambling debts, or backdated child support payments are the most pressing.

I had an ex-boyfriend who owed some dodgy characters in London money and he came home with a new broken finger every few days. It cost him the use of his hands for a while and one girlfriend when it became painfully obvious to me that he was mixed up in something he shouldn't be. That's an expensive debt. If he were a smart man, he would have paid that one off first or read the terms and conditions more thoroughly before getting involved. I am assuming for the sake of brevity that you are more sensible than him, but if not for God's sake pay off the gangsters first. Then proceed to the banks.

Somewhere on each of these statements should be a line that tells you how much you have paid in interest on each debt. It's probably in small print and it may be on the last page but it's there. If it's zero then congratulations, my friend, you're perfect! If not (and this is most of us) circle it and take a moment to think about this number. Don't beat yourself up; just think about what you are going to spend this money on next year instead of credit card interest. Remember, we are not berating ourselves for our past behaviors here. We are just acknowledging that we have paid too much in interest, but that's not what we are going to do anymore. From now on this very same money is going toward your goals!

Figure out how to reduce the amount of interest you are paying.

The next step is to look at how you can reduce the amount of interest you are paying. There are several ways to do this. One might be opening a new credit card with a 0% interest introductory rate and transferring the balance from your other credit cards (starting with the one with the highest interest rate) onto it. Alternatively you might take out a personal loan to pay off all of your other debts—a loan that charges a lower rate than what you are cumulatively paying now. If neither of those options work then you could also look at transferring all or part of the balance from the card with the highest interest rate onto the card with the lowest interest rate. Whether you manage to save 20% or 2% on the interest rate that you are paying on your debt, that is going to free up some cash that was otherwise slipping down the drain, so pat yourself on the back and tell yourself what a good girl or boy you are.

Interest savings are exponential, not linear.

Reorganizing your debt in this way has huge benefits at very little cost to you, but because the numbers are exponential rather than linear—in other words, rather vague—many of us underestimate the value of doing so. Studies have shown that people who are merely told the percentage in interest that they will save are only somewhat likely to follow through with refinancing their debt. Those who are told the figure in a dollar amount are more likely to, and those who are shown the difference in a graph are the most likely to invest the necessary time to optimize their debt. If you have the time, feel free to create such a graph for yourself. If not, just make the decision that you don't want to waste even one extra dollar unnecessarily on interest and commit to reorganizing your debt today.

Focus on reducing your highest-interest borrowing, not the number of debts that you have.

Another setback that we must overcome was discovered in a series of psychological experiments that showed how bad we humans are naturally at managing our debt. Even the most financially savvy are tempted to pay off the smallest debts first rather than focusing on those with the highest interest rates. This is because we are naturally "debt account averse;" in other words, we are more motivated to reduce the number of debts that we have than reduce the total cost. By reorganizing our debts before attempting to repay them, we can often fulfill our desire to reduce the number of accounts that we hold in a much more financially efficient way. Just remember not to close accounts that you have attained a $0 balance on. We will talk more about credit scores later, but keeping these open (but paid off) will improve your score. Just be sure to chop up the cards so you aren't tempted to use them.

Warning! Your brain will not want to collaborate on this project!

Facing the reality of your debts is likely to provoke some level of anxiety, which quiets the thinking part of your brain and activates the reptilian part. The reptilian part will use all of its tricks to prevent you from doing the work necessary to take action here. It will use its warped sense of time to tell you that you're too busy right now to research the options. It will take *hours*, it warns, when in reality you should be done in thirty minutes. It uses the same tactics on you when it doesn't want you to unload the dishwasher. You've been here before; you are strong enough to ignore it and make those phone calls.

Depending on the size of your debt, you could end up saving hundreds if not thousands in the half hour that you are about to dedicate to this. That's pretty good compensation for a few phone calls. How are you going to redirect that money toward your goals?

If you are not sure where to start with this, there are plenty of confidential debt counseling services that will help you to consolidate or re-finance your debt for free. Your bank also may offer free financial counseling, or if you are more of a do-it-yourselfer, you can simply apply for a couple of personal loans online (not too many as it could affect your credit) or look for a credit card that offers a 0% interest rate for the first year, onto which you can roll your existing debts. Try not to do this more times in your lifetime than you really need to as opening new accounts too frequently will negatively affect your credit score too. This is a good fix if you plan to pay down your debt aggressively.

Confidence comes from commitment, not experience. You can do this!

If you are still hesitating, then take a moment to examine what feelings you are experiencing that are holding you back. Refinancing seems complex and you may find yourself thinking that you *don't know how to do it*. When we don't feel experienced enough to do something, we often don't have the confidence to do it. But really, confidence comes from *commitment*, not experience. If you simply commit yourself to calling a debt counselor or inquiring about personal loans or a new credit card, the confidence will follow. You will figure it out.

And remember, don't pressure yourself into finding the perfect option. This will lead to decision paralysis where you become so fearful of making the wrong decision that you can't bring yourself to make one at all. The goal here is simply to find a better option than you currently have. You can always adjust your plan as you go. Just remember we are looking to create lots of small changes in our financial picture in order to make a big impact. If you reduce the interest that you are paying even by 1% then you did a good thing for yourself.

Start paying down your debt.

Congratulations on optimizing your debts and committing to paying less interest to the banks. Take the interest that you will be saving and increase the direct deposit for one of your goals by that amount. You won't miss that money as it was already disappearing from your account each month. Now let's work on reducing your interest payments even further by paying down your debt.

The first step to success is accountability. Yes, there may have been dire circumstances or this debt may even have been a very sensible investment (such as a student loan), but you still *chose* to get into debt and now you are *choosing* to get out of it. When you look at it that way, it is empowering.

Set up direct debits for all debt repayments.

To start paying down your debt, set up direct deposits for the monthly minimum payment for each card. This will prevent a moment of forgetfulness from costing you in late fees. Then calculate how much more you can afford to pay and apply it *all* to the debt that charges the highest interest rate on the borrowing. Just remember that paying the minimum payments on the rest of the debts is only a temporary measure. If you continue to pay just the minimum amount due indefinitely, it will take you approximately 300 years and a firstborn child to pay off your debt and all the while that 16.9% APR will keep on compounding.

According to FINRA's National Financial Capability study, one-third of Americans pay only the minimum amount due on their credit cards every month and that means that a lot of us are funding the extravagant lifestyles of the banks' CEOs and not our own. Ever wondered how those credit card companies are able to offer such generous perks? It's because statistically you will be paying them back three times over in interest. I like to schedule a calendar reminder every month to check my credit card bill a few days before it is due to come out of my account so that I can make sure I have the maximum amount I can afford ready to pay it off. Depending on how you get paid you can also schedule this reminder every two weeks. That might fit better if you get paid twice a month or if you want to start working on increasing your credit score.

Paying off large debts will tax your motivation heavily.

The bad news, if you have a lot of debt, is that when it comes to undertaking any task we humans are highly susceptible to a phenomenon called Temporal Motivation Theory, an integrative motivational theory developed by Piers Steel and Cornelius J. König.

The theory is that our motivation increases as our confidence of achieving a certain goal or outcome increases. By the same token our motivation is reduced when there is a large amount of time (delay) expected before the reward is realized. So if you have a large debt and are aware that it will take months or even years to pay it off, you are likely to struggle to stay motivated.

Dave Ramsey, the well-known financial guru, capitalizes on this theory by advising his followers to pay off the smallest debts first, regardless of interest rate. This certainly works psychologically. After all, it is easier to motivate yourself to cook at home for a month in order to pay off the last $500 on your car loan than it is to commit to the same strategy to make a $500 payment on a seemingly bottomless $50,000 credit card debt. Mathematically, however, you end up paying more interest on your total debt over the long run.

Make your own milestones and create a reward system.

A better way to capitalize on Temporal Motivation theory in my opinion is to optimize your debt in terms of the interest paid by refinancing or consolidating as discussed above. It will give you a nice mental boost by reducing the number of your accounts. Then break down your debt repayment into bite-sized chunks and sweeten the deal for yourself with rewards along the way. Ignore the bigger picture, which is your total debt, and instead put it into your calendar in terms of milestones. These should be achievable so if you make $40k per year and have $100k in debt you should have a strategy that spans multiple years.

Take your total debt, decide how long you want to give yourself to pay it off, and then divide the debt by the number of months—finally set up a direct deposit to automate these contributions. As well as benefitting from the "set it and forget it" mentality, this will ensure that you never miss a payment, a mistake that the credit card companies would gleefully charge you for. Then choose your rewards and the frequency with which you want to treat yourself and schedule those in the calendar. If you know you only have to pay down $203 more to earn a spa day or a bottle of your favorite Scotch, you will find you can more easily turn down an impulse purchase.

By taking advantage of the surge of motivation that you will experience as you near each milestone and its reward, you can make paying off your debt a much less painful experience and maintain your motivation for the long haul.

Just remember, if you start investing the money that you used to spend on credit card interest over your lifetime, you can build yourself a tidy fortune, depending on your level of debt. The average American household with credit card debt pays $1,292 per year in interest. That's $12,920 down the drain over a 10-year period. Talk about opportunity cost! If you invested those annual payments for 10 years at an 8% rate of return you would have $20,213.96.

Yes, giving up luxuries can be challenging, but surely giving up paying big bucks to credit card companies is a no-brainer. Grab a sticker or a piece of painter's tape and write yourself a note on the front of your credit card. This could pertain to one of your goals or to your retirement plans. I find "Cruises, not cat food" to be pretty motivating.

Keep paid-off debt accounts open.

Once you are done paying off each credit card (yay for you!), by all means chop them up, burn them at the stake, or repurpose them as snow scrapers for your windshield, but do not close the account. We will discuss why in the chapter about improving your credit score. I have read several articles that suggest freezing those naughty cards into a block of ice so that if you urgently need them they are still there. I would agree that a good test of whether you really, really need to buy something is if you are willing to spend three hours licking your credit cards out of an ice block. However, maybe limit it to just one card. Having four available for emergencies seems excessive.

You didn't get into debt in a day and you probably won't get out of it in a day. Well, unless your debt is very small or you win the lottery. The important thing is to make a start and then keep moving forward. If you have to take baby steps at first, so be it. If a time arises that you can start taking flying leaps, do it! If something goes wrong, don't give up. Go back to the baby steps for a while but just keep moving. Sometimes it is important to forget the big picture (particularly if it is terrifying) and just put one foot in front of the other.

The great Forrest Gump once said:

"That day, for no particular reason, I decided to go for a little run. So I ran to the end of the road. And when I got there, I thought maybe I'd run to the end of town. And when I got there, I thought maybe I'd just run across Greenbow County. And I figured, since I run this far, maybe I'd just run across the great state of Alabama. And that's what I did. I ran clear across Alabama."

Think of your debt as Alabama, but just start with a little run. No offense to Alabama, but just think how good you will feel to have run clear across it and out the other side.

ACTION STEPS

1. Refinance or consolidate your debt to reduce the amount of interest that you have to pay on it.

2. Make yourself a payment plan for your debt and create rewards along the way.

3. Automate your repayment plan so you never get another late fee.

4. Remember the sheet we created in the beginning of your book listing your assets, liabilities, income, savings, and expenses? Pull it out of your folder and see if you have assets or savings available to you that you could apply to your debt now to save on interest.

Download my free Debt Reduction Party Worksheet from my website ThisisYourBrainonMoney.com.

Chapter Summary

- Saving money on interest costs you nothing in terms of your lifestyle.

- Prioritize reducing the amount of money you pay in interest, not the number of debt accounts you have.

- Confidence comes from commitment, not experience.

- Don't give yourself analysis paralysis. Your goal is not to find the perfect solution, just a better one than you currently have.

-Start paying down debts, starting with the most expensive, and automate these payments so you never pay another late fee.

- Create a reward system for yourself based on milestones of your choosing.

- Ignore the big picture and focus instead on small gains.

CHAPTER 7
BAD DEBT VS.
GOOD DEBT

There are two types of debt, Bad Debt and Good Debt, and in the previous chapter we focused on the bad. Good Debt might be a mortgage, student loans, or a loan for an investment with a good interest rate. This type of debt serves a higher purpose, allowing you to invest in your home or yourself. The interest on it is often tax-deductible, and the idea is that it allows you to finance something that should eventually increase in value. I would add that a good debt should also be affordable. If you end up buying a house that is $200k over your budget and struggle with the repayments, then while the first portion of your loan is definitely good debt, the extra $200k on the loan falls into the category of a bad debt. Student loans spent on a degree that turns out to be less than desirable in terms of the job market might also be considered a bad debt.

Smart debt frees up spare cash for better things.

Smart debt, a sort of subset of Good Debt, is debt when you don't technically need to borrow but have chosen to do so for financial gain in another area. An example of this might be in the way that someone purchases a car. Now let's imagine you have an extra $40k sitting in the bank. Wouldn't that be nice? Treat yourself by imagining it for a few more minutes. You might, considering the general consensus that debt is bad, think that the most prudent way to purchase your next ride is to use that $40k buy it free and clear. Wrong! Because if you can get a great deal on a car loan (at say 2% interest) then you would be better off investing that cash in a product that will give you a return higher than 2%. Depending on your risk tolerance that could be a money market account, a CD (where the money is tied up for a certain amount of time), or in stocks or bonds.

Determining whether a debt is "smart" or not involves considering the opportunity cost of dedicating a large chunk of money to purchase something that could be paid for in smaller increments. Put simply, it means taking out a loan at a low interest rate so that you can funnel your spare cash into something that pays you more in returns, increases in value, or both. It sounds like a no-brainer but actually there are some issues to consider here. The most pressing would be whether you can afford the monthly payments on any loans you take out once that big chunk of cash is tied up. Secondly it requires having a chunk of cash lying around in the first place.

It also involves cojones*, or "risk tolerance" as they say in smart circles. If you have grandes co-jones (and a big bank balance) then you could take Smart Debt one step further and use it to get into more debt. Double Smart Debt!

Assuming the same scenario of having that spare $40k in the bank (spare meaning in addition to your savings) and needing a new car, an example of Double Smart Debt might be taking out a loan to purchase your car and using the $40k as a down payment on a $200k rental property. In other words, using your smart debt to take on another debt. The idea being that the property would not only increase in value but could generate a monthly income. Sounds fantastic, right? Well it might be, but you would need to do some serious math first. You would now have two sizeable pay-ments to make every month, and rental property is a rather fickle income source. Would you be able to meet your financial obligations if the property were to remain vacant, for example?

Assuming that, like most of us, you don't have a huge chunk of investable cash lying around, let's focus on some ways that you might be able to save on the Good Debt that you have acquired.

*Alex said that it is unprofessional to say "balls," so I changed it to "cojones" to sound more sophisticated.

Consider your car loan.

We briefly talked about car loans but now let's go a little deeper as car loans tend to be the largest debt that most people who don't own a house have.

Your car is a depreciating asset.

While it might be considered a good debt in that your car serves a purpose (getting you from A to B) and usually car loans have relatively low interest rates, what many of us fail to think about is that unlike your house, your car is a textbook example of a *depreciating asset*. Its value drops every year, and the more expensive the car, the higher the depreciation. A $75,000 Ferrari, to give an example on the more extreme end of the scale, would depreciate by about $8,000 per year. This means just to *maintain* your net worth you would need to squirrel an additional $8,000 into your savings every year.

So while it might be tempting to see a nice car as a reasonable reward for all of your hard work, if the reason that you go into the office in the first place is to increase your net worth, then it is counterproductive.

Ideally you want to buy a reliable secondhand car with an affordable car payment and drive it for as long after you finish paying it off as possible. A vast car payment not only takes a huge chunk out of your investable income (i.e., money that you can put to work making more money), but it is also a ball and chain, compelling you to make certain lifestyle choices; i.e., staying at a job you hate or passing up on traveling. It can also be an enormous stressor should your financial circumstances change and you find yourself struggling to make the payments. When I got divorced and joined an online dating website, I aggressively swiped left on anyone posing in or next to their convertible sports car because:

A) I could already tell they were going to be a douche. It's okay to own a fancy car but putting it on your dating profile? Yuck!

B) I didn't trust their financial decision-making and I'm not going to eat cat food as an old lady for anyone. And…

C) Open-top cars mess my hair up.

If your car payment is eating into your savings goals, consider trading down.

If I have reached you too late and you are already saddled with a vast chunk of car debt and have other financial concerns, then consider selling or trading in your ride for something more modest, particularly if the current ride is a gas-guzzler as well as a cash-guzzler. I understand that this isn't easy. An old roommate of mine drove a fabulous Beamer that she had financed when she started her first job. It was shiny and luxurious and when you closed the door it played a wonderful *brrrring* sound to remind you that you were rich. We loved it. We swished around town like a pair of movie stars sitting on towels so that our fake tan didn't mark the leather seats.

When I look back on that time of my life, the car played a large part in how glamorous it all felt. Unfortunately my roommate's job wasn't as great a success as the car and she started to seriously hate it. She was unable to leave, however, because the car payment (which amounted to several hundred dollars) needed to be paid and she didn't have enough savings to cover it while she looked for a new job. Weeks of misery followed and the car rather lost its shine, the *brrring* sound mocking her every time she got in it.

Choose your luxuries and establish whether your car makes the cut.

I will discuss the concept in more detail a little bit later, but I am a firm believer in choosing your luxuries. If cars truly are your passion or if your job requires presenting an image of affluence (e.g., sales) then there could be an argument for driving a luxury car. If this applies to you and you like to upgrade every four years or so then it might actually make sense to lease rather than own.

If you are going to lease, however, be smart about it. Make sure you aren't going to exceed the allowed annual mileage (a very costly mistake) and don't add any dealer-installed upgrades (rims, sound system, etc.) as in reality you will be renting, not buying those too. Be sure to take out "gap insurance" so that if you total the car you won't have to pay the difference between what the insurance company deems fair market value and what the dealer considers that figure to be (spoiler alert, it is almost always more). And lastly, crunch the real numbers before committing. In addition to the advertised monthly fee, you will pay a deposit at the beginning and a turn-in fee at the end. Also, you will be liable for taxes on the monthly payments, registration, and any damage fees should the car take a scrape.

Kit your budget car out with "luxury" accessories.

If you are nearing the end of this section and still teetering on the fence about downgrading a ride that you really can't afford because you can't give up all of those bells and whistles then I have a few more tips. You can get an iPad holder for $15 for your kids to watch movies on, a new sound system, a remote starter, or even a heated backrest that plugs into the USB socket. Game changer.

If you need a backup camera or assisted parking, borrow a ten-year-old. There is nothing that mine enjoys more than yelling "Oh my God you are going to hit that car AND THE PEOPLE ARE IN IT!" Okay, maybe "enjoy" is the wrong word, but she seems to do it a lot and it saves me from straining my neck to look behind me when I reverse.

Whatever you do, don't skip on maintenance. Properly maintained cars can last 200,000 miles and beyond. Certain makes, such as Toyota and Honda, have particularly good reputations when it comes to longevity so bear this in mind when picking out a new ride.

Continue to drive your car after it is paid off.

Finally, please enjoy the benefits of a paid-off car for a few years before upgrading. So many of us rush to the car lot for an upgrade as soon as one vehicle is paid off when it would be so much more productive to put the money that you are saving on a car payment to use in your retirement account or savings. This is a large monthly outlay, usually several hundred dollars. It wouldn't take long to convert that saving into a fully stocked emergency fund or a regular contribution to your retirement fund.

Student loans are a good debt so long as the degree makes you employable.

Student loans are undeniably a good debt, providing that you are investing in a degree that will open the door to real life job opportunities and that you are determined and passionate about pursuing. Yes, there are a few wildly successful art historians, but they are the exception rather than the rule. While we all should follow our dreams and pursue our passions, for most people with creative genes, a business degree will serve you better in the long run, allowing you to turn your gifts into a thriving enterprise generating cold, hard cash. You can minor in the artsy stuff or take classes outside of college. A few hours of research into degrees that will make you both employable and earning a rate that sounds agreeable to you could save you from an extremely costly mistake. Plus, the outcome of an investment in yourself is easier to control.

If you are young enough not to have gone to college yet, then first off congratulations for educating yourself on your finances before you have the chance to screw them all up. I would have signed up for a bank loan at 600% APR in exchange for a free pen in college. Thank God my campus was so small the banks and credit card companies didn't bother setting up shop there. Young people are often seen as easy targets due to their propensity to not read or not understand the small print and their inability to resist freebies. Be smarter! If you are in the process of applying to or attending college then consider the following ideas to save some money.

Apply for lots of scholarships.

First off, apply for as many scholarships as you possibly can. That's free money that you don't need to pay back. Spend a day researching and putting yourself forward for everything that you might be eligible for. If you are accepted for even one of them then you just made hundreds, maybe even thousands in a few hours. How cool is that? You just made the same paycheck as a lawyer and you don't even have a degree yet. Simply type "Find Scholarships for College" into Google and then try one of the search engines that list offerings for different schools in the country. It's seriously worth a shot.

Put paying down school loans on the back burner.

If college is a distant memory for you and the task that remains is paying off the rest of your debts, then do so but prioritize your other debts first. The interest on student loans is tax deductible so assuming that you earn enough to take advantage of this then it's not a bad debt to have.

Mortgage debt is fabulous.

This is a debt that we should all aspire to. As well as providing a tax deduction in the form of interest, providing you pick a good property, the bank is lending you a vast sum of money to invest in a commodity that should increase in value for a very low interest rate. No one is lining up to lend you $300k at 4% to invest in the stock market, but they will do it for a house. Even if your property doesn't appreciate as you had hoped, you still get to keep those monthly payments in the form of an asset (your house), rather than letting them disappear into someone else's pocket as we do when we rent.

Mortgage debt is a great place to look for big savings.

This being said, a loan of such a high amount even with a relatively low interest rate means a big opportunity to overpay or, if you are smart, save. If you haven't bought a home yet, then the best thing that you can possibly do is to optimize your credit score, and I will explain how to do that in the next chapter. The interest rate that you pay on your mortgage is dependent on your credit score, and while the difference can look minimal on paper, it makes a huge difference in real life due to the size of the loan.

If you already have a mortgage then it isn't too late to benefit from a great credit score. If yours has improved since you bought your house or you take a few months to bump it up, then it is worth looking into refinancing. A few extra points on the credit score can make all the difference. As can a fall in mortgage rates on a national level. Take a couple of hours to look into your mortgage and ensure that you are getting the best rate possible. Before refinancing just be careful to make sure that the cumulative savings on your monthly payment will exceed the cost of refinancing. If you plan to move in a couple of years, it may not be worth it. Calculating the break-even point is key.

Next look at how much you have paid off on your mortgage and how much you have left to go. When the size of your loan is comparatively small in terms of the equity that you have built, then that may also allow you to get a lower rate.

One final way to save money on your mortgage is to pay it off early. If you pay it off in 15 rather than 30 years, that would be a huge saving on the interest that you would pay on the loan. However, remember when we discussed Smart Debt? A mortgage is a great example of this. Most people pay between 3.5 and 5.5% on their mortgage, which is lower than the return that we might expect from some other types of investments. So it doesn't necessarily make sense to tie up all of your assets in your house. As well as investing in the stock market you could consider putting money into other real estate such as rental properties or commercial investments. Again, this all depends on your risk tolerance, and for some people, the security of a paid-off home is worth the opportunity cost of a more volatile investment strategy.

There is such a thing as good credit card debt.

We spent most of the last chapter aiming to wipe out our credit card debt, so it may come as a surprise to hear that credit card debt could, in some sense, be considered good. My goal for you when it comes to credit cards is not in fact to make you swear off them for life. It's to have you adjust the way you view them. They are not tools to purchase things that you can't afford, as the evil marketing people have persuaded us. If you use them in lieu of cash and pay off the full balance every month, then you can take advantage of the many perks such as free insurance, cash back, and loyalty points. When used mindfully they are also a great tool to maximize your credit score. My philosophy isn't like Alcoholics Anonymous; I don't expect you to commit to terminal credit card sobriety. I simply want you to be able to enjoy a couple of glasses of champagne at a wedding without urinating in the font.

If you make sure to pay off your balance in full every month, then you will be able to take advantage of the attractive perks that credit cards offer without falling into their evil debt trap. I use one credit card for most of my purchases. It collects air miles for me, and by putting almost everything on it and paying the balance down to zero every month, it allows me to fly to the motherland once a year to hang out with my tea-swilling, crumpet-munching chums. Notice that I said "balance" here, not "bill." The bill is what you owe for the previous month's borrowing. The balance is what you owe up to this moment. If you spend $3,000 per month on your credit card and pay off only the bill for last month, then you still owe $3,000 for this month and they will charge you interest for the pleasure. If you pay off the balance you will have racked up $0 in interest. Just make sure that the annual fee that the card charges doesn't eclipse the benefits that you gain from using it.

Action Steps

1. See if there is a way for you to use Smart Debt to free up spare cash for better investments.

2. Do an inventory of your "good debt" to make sure that none of it is bad debt in disguise, then ensure that you aren't overspending on it.

3. Cars are a depreciating asset. Examine whether yours is a worthwhile debt. If it isn't, trade down.

4. If you are applying to or in college, search for ways to reduce the number of loans you take out and apply for as many scholarships as you can.

5. Examine your mortgage and ensure you are paying the lowest interest rate possible.

Chapter Summary

- Bad debt is a drain on your finances, but good debt allows you to optimize your finances.

- Your car is a depreciating asset so purchase it with great care and consider leasing if a luxury car is a necessity for you. Second hand is the only way to go whatever type of car you buy as a brand new one will plummet in value the moment you drive it off the lot.

- Your student loans will only be a good debt if they make you employable.

- Explore scholarships to reduce the amount of student debt you accrue

- Mortgage debt is good so long as it is affordable. Due to the size of the loan the stakes are high, which means there are huge opportunities to overpay if you choose badly or save money if you choose wisely.

- Credit card debt is great if you can make it interest free by paying the full balance off every month.

CHAPTER 8 HOW TO INCREASE YOUR CREDIT SCORE

Hopefully the last chapter got you pretty excited about saving money and paying down debt and you've been eagerly calculating all of the extra green that you're going to cling to in the next year. Well, here comes the big panty-dropper. What if I told you that I am going to teach you how to save tens of thousands of dollars in this chapter? The best part is that it doesn't involve making your own crappy sandwiches or forgoing lattes!

Cutting out lattes isn't the secret to

financial success.

Confession: I wrote this while I was drinking a $5 rosewater latte in an extremely trendy café. As I mentioned earlier, I like to condition myself to enjoy productive habits such as working on my book by giving myself a little treat as I am a good golden retriever—I mean girl—and I deserve it!

I was doing my best to relax and submit to the delectable flavor of the perfectly roasted, floral-scented treat, but the voices of every writer who has ever written about finance kept interrupting my thoughts. According to them, buying coffee outside of the home is the dirtiest financial habit in existence. It is the sex without a condom of spending. It has, if you believe the hype, caused us to burden our parents financially years after we should have become independent, kept us from buying our own homes, and caused us to spend nearly $2,000 per year without noticing.

Technically the last part may be true, and if you are buying expensive coffee every single day you should probably stop. However, Ramit Sethi makes an excellent point in his book *I Will Teach You to Be Rich* when he says that there is something else that will end up costing us infinitely more than a latte habit. And if only the financial experts could shut up about lattes long enough to mention it, we might well be able move out of our mom's basements.

Your credit score could end up costing you tens of thousands of dollars.

I don't know how much you know about credit scores, but I will assume you know nothing. One tiny element of your score may be all that is standing between you and the "Excellent" category, so I will cover all of the basics in the hope that you can unearth the missing piece of the puzzle.

Your credit score is based on your borrowing history, and businesses use it to determine whether they want to lend you money. What they also use it to determine is how great of a risk you are to lend to, and with that in mind, how much interest they need to charge you to make that risk worthwhile. Given that most of us will or at least would like to buy a house at some point in our life, and that requires borrowing hundreds of thousands of dollars, then the interest rate that we are going to pay on future borrowing is pretty bloody important.

To put this into context, someone with a great FICO score of between 760-850 would pay 4.364% APR on a 30-year fixed $300,000 mortgage. Someone with a less impressive FICO score of 620-639 would pay 5.953% APR on the same mortgage. The first person is saving 1.589% in interest on their loan! Okay, that doesn't sound like much. I hinted at a panty-dropper and this doesn't seem like it. Until you figure out that this means over the lifetime of the loan the second person is paying $105,727 more than the first person! Lawd Jesus have mercy! Do you really want to donate $105k of your hard-earned cash to the CEO of your bank's golfing fund?

Think for a minute how long you have to work at your crappy job to make $105k, then promise yourself you will start optimizing your credit score today to get the best interest rates possible on your mortgage. You could retire a year or more early with a saving like that! Or install a pool complete with a waterslide, underwater speakers, and hot pool boys (or girls) in your $300k house! Screw it, you could buy a $400k house instead of a $300k house and have an extra bedroom.

To make a comparable saving in coffee, you would need to not drink 21,145 lattes over the same 30-year period. That's 704 per year or nearly two per day. Given that working on your credit score is almost twice as effective as giving up your daily latte, the financial experts ought to be shouting about it from the rooftops of all the newsrooms. So why the hell do they keep banging on about our coffee habits instead? Because they are jealous, that's why. They are as jealous and bitter as their cup of cheap office coffee. Or perhaps it is because talking about credit scores isn't considered as sexy? I can't think why not. There is nothing that revs my motor more than a mysterious, dark stranger with a bulging credit score and $105k more to spend on wooing me over the next 30 years. In fact, Alex told me his credit score during our initial Tinder exchange. This makes him sound super weird, but to be fair I was demanding all of his other vital statistics so I could run a background check before I met him in person. You know, in case he was a murderer. I didn't actually ask for his credit score, but as any woman who has ever tried online dating knows, sometimes men show you big things over the Internet even if you didn't ask to see them. And to be fair, it was very impressive.

Check your credit report today.

So how do you measure up? Legally, you are allowed a free copy of your credit report from each of the big three credit reporting agencies once a year, so if you haven't already done so, order your copies online from AnnualCreditReport.com right now (this won't affect your score). Instead of asking for them all at once, you can have one sent every four months so you can keep tabs on your financial health throughout the year. According to a survey from CreditCards.com half of Americans haven't checked their report in the last six months, but guess who the most likely age group to have checked it was? Latte-swigging Millennials! So take that, haters. We are more on top of our finances than those old farts would have us believe. In fact, 18% of American adults have never checked their credit score, so by taking this one small step you are leaping ahead of them.

Sit down, pour yourself three fingers of organic, small batch java, and read through your credit report carefully, checking for are any inaccuracies. I check my score fairly regularly on Mint.com, but I experienced a sudden 38-point drop when a student loan that I paid off in 2014 was mysteriously added back to the debts that I owed. If you find anything amiss, then you need to call the agencies and have them look into it.

Your credit score is calculated on several criteria.

The first factor affecting your score is on-time payments. Remember when I told you to set up a direct debit for the minimum amount due on your credit card each month? Here is another very good reason to follow through with that. As well as costing you money in outrageous penalty fees, a missed payment will hit your credit score and therefore affect the amount that you pay in interest on future borrowings. Always set up automatic payments for your bills. Put a calendar reminder the day before they draw in case you need to adjust the amount or beg the company you owe for an extension. And don't forget, you can call most companies and ask to have your bill paid on the day of your choosing. Having the money draw on or just after payday is much more convenient than having it due three days before payday.

The second factor affecting your credit score is *how many accounts* you have. A few years ago I thought I was doing great by keeping it simple, having only one credit card and paying that off regularly. This was true to an extent because my borrowing was easy to keep track of and never got out of control. However, lenders see this as a "thin file," which means that there is not enough evidence of good borrowing. Ideally they like to see a mixture of debts, such as a car loan, credit card, and a student loan, all with clockwork payments. More than one credit card is also a plus, so if you have only one or no credit cards then consider applying for a second. Assuming, that is, that you trust yourself to control your spending. Don't just apply for any card, though. We are regularly bombarded with offers in the mail and online all with tempting introductory offers. Think of these as potential Tinder dates. Good cards are friends with benefits. Bad cards are serial killers. Ideally you will find the Tinder unicorn: a card that takes care of you for life. This is especially valuable because the longevity of your credit accounts is another important factor.

After much deliberation I upped my credit score by applying for a second credit card. I knew that I wasn't really going to use this credit card as I prefer to collect my British Airways miles and therefore I wasn't going to benefit much from the rewards. An annual fee would therefore be an expense that I wasn't going to make back in perks. I went for the Costco credit card that doesn't charge a fee if you have a Costco membership, which I do (and you should too). I set up a few direct debits to draw from it, as it is important not just to *have* the card but also to *use* it. I made sure these were for static amounts, so Hulu, Verizon, etc., rather than a fluctuating electricity bill. Then I set up an automatic payment to pay that balance off in full every month so I never had to think about it again. As well as helping my score by fattening out my skinny file (which Costco also does to my waistline with its vast wheels of French cheese) it helped me with the fourth factor in calculating credit scores: Credit Utilization Rate.

This is where my score was really hurting. Your credit utilization score is how much you borrow out of the credit that you have. My one credit card had a limit of $5,000 and I tended to use about $3,000 of that each month before paying off the entire balance. Responsible, right? Well, not enough to please FICO. Regularly spending $3,000 or my $5,000 limit put me at 60% in terms of credit utilization when ideally one should be below 30%. Thankfully there are simple solutions to this problem.

First off I had applied for that second card, which had another $5,000 limit. This meant that I now had a $10,000 credit limit. The same $3,000 per month of borrowing now put me right at 30% without my having to change a thing. Then I looked further into the whole credit utilization shtick and discovered that as well as looking at your overall use of credit, some companies look at how much you borrow at any one time on a single card. Dang it! Well, there was another easy solution for this, it turned out. I started paying off my card twice a month instead of once. Now without any change in my actual spending habits I had decreased my overall credit utilization from 60% to

30% with the second card and from 30% to 15% by paying everything off twice per month instead of once.

Then, because I had a taste for the credit reporting agency's blood, I went in for the kill and asked for a credit increase on my trusty old British Airways card. As I had been a good and consistent customer, they didn't hesitate to raise it to $12,000. Now suddenly I had a credit limit of $17,000 and was carrying a maximum balance of about $1,500 at any one time, which put me at a 9% credit card utilization score. Schwing! Without changing a thing about my spending habits, I had cunningly disguised myself as a much more responsible human.

Now if you are unable to use one or more of these tips to improve your score, then I have two final tricks up my sleeve for you. You can call your credit card company and ask them on what day they report to the credit reporting agencies. They usually do this monthly, but it doesn't always coincide with the day that the bill hits your doormat (or inbox). Find out the day, mark it in your calendar, and pay all or as much as you possibly can, right before this.

Lastly, if you are young and have no credit history at all, it may help you to have a co-signer on your first account. This could be a parent, partner, or very good friend. When I first moved to America

I found myself in that boat as all of my credit had been built in a foreign country. I would have seriously struggled to get any loans or cards, but fortunately for me the British Airways card took into account my UK credit when deciding whether or not to lend to me in America. So that is an option if you come from abroad. Credit card companies that collect miles for a foreign airline may be more inclined to look into your credit score from your home country.

ACTION STEPS

1. Log onto a free credit monitoring website such as Mint.com to check your score and take whatever steps are necessary to maximize it.

2. Automate all bill payments so you never miss one again.

Chapter Summary

- Your latte habit is insignificant compared to the savings you can make over a lifetime by maximizing your credit score.

- You can (and should) check your credit score for free.

- Your credit score is calculated using the following criteria: your history of on-time payments, the number of open accounts you have, your credit utilization rate, and the length of time each account has been open.

- There are several tricks you can use to maximize your credit score without changing your spending habits.

CHAPTER 9 HOW TO LOOK LIKE A GROWN-UP (ON PAPER)

This chapter is very practical and provides a checklist of everything you need to set up be a true grown-up in the financial sense. For most of us, this checklist will be a work in progress, but if you take the time to at least set up these accounts you can fund them over time using the tips and habits you picked up in the previous chapters.

I went to a free consultation with a financial advisor at my bank before I met Alex and he disclosed that 99% of his clients do not have all of these items in place. Want to join the 1% with me? Of course you do! These steps are easy to take and will propel you toward financial success. The action items in this chapter shouldn't take long to complete and, boy, will you feel accomplished afterwards. When you meet with a financial advisor, they will go over these items with you so it's nice to have a basic understanding of them beforehand. It will make your meeting go much more smoothly and will free up time to talk about more interesting stuff.

1. **An Emergency Fund.** This should be in a separate account from your checking and should contain three to six months of expenses should you get fired from your job or otherwise lose your income. This sounds like an intimidating sum and it is. You won't save this up in a day, but you can start contributing to it today.

Calculate how much you spend in a month including mortgage/rent, utilities, food, gas, and miscellaneous expenses. Then set up a direct deposit every month to start funding this goal. You should aim to earn a reasonable amount of interest on your emergency fund savings, as we are talking about a fairly large sum of money. However, you don't want a great amount of volatility or risk, as you may need those funds at short notice. You also need relatively easy access, although not so easy that you are tempted to borrow inappropriately from it.

A high-yield savings account is one idea. You will need to do some serious shopping around, though, as interest rates range from 0.09% to around 2%. An online bank that doesn't offer brick and mortar services may offer a better rate than a traditional one. Be sure to check that the fees are low and there are no or very low penalties for withdrawing money.

Another idea, particularly if you already have a stocked emergency fund, might be a money market account. Some have fees or require a minimum balance so you will need to do a little research here. The advantage is that they offer debit card and check services, which can be handy for paying unexpected expenses. The interest rate paid out fluctuates along with the market so it is worth considering where you think those interest rates will go. Most forecasters suggest a lazy increase over the next couple of years due to creeping core inflation.

As of February 2020, certificates of deposit (CDs) tend to offer slightly higher rates of interest (around 2-2.3%) than online savings accounts (around 1.7%) and Money Market accounts (around 1.7%). However, they require a time commitment and there are penalties for early withdrawal. If you decide to go for this option then consider "laddering" them. This means splitting your money into separate CDs that mature at different times. For example, one might be in a six-month CD, another in a one-year one, and a third in a three-year one. None of these options should be considered investments, though, as they are likely to grow at a slower pace than the rate of inflation (currently at 2.74%), but they do at least offer a safe place to stash the cash that you want to keep on hand for emergencies.

The final option is to purchase treasury bills with your emergency fund money. Treasury bills are short-term debt obligations of the US government. You generally purchase them at less than face value and then sell them at the full price when they mature. The length of time that they take to mature varies from days to years and they come in increments of $100. Although they need to mature to be sold at full value, you can sell them before that for cash in a pinch so they do offer some flexibility.

2. **Bad Surprise Fund.** As well as an emergency fund for a total disaster, such as income loss, I like to have a smaller emergency fund on hand for unexpected events such as the transmission going out

in my car, the water heater breaking, or certain expected but irregular expenses such as new tires. This is optional, but throwing $100 into it every month keeps my anxiety down. If you find that you aren't using it very often, you can funnel any surplus funds into your retirement accounts.

3. **Retirement Accounts.** You will want to discuss the specifics of these with a financial advisor, but the sooner you start contributing to a retirement account the better. If you have a job with benefits, ensure that you are at the very least contributing the maximum amount that your employer will match to your 401k. This is an employer-sponsored retirement plan that employees can contribute to through automatic payroll withholding. The employer may match some or all of those contributions, and that means free money for you, which is always the best kind.

I will share tips for choosing a financial advisor in the next chapter, but I want you to whip out your calendar right now and set a time in a couple of days to make a few calls and set up some meetings. If you are not ready to meet with a financial advisor just yet, then online robo-advisors such as Betterment, Ell-vest or Vanguard offer great tools for doing it yourself. You can literally set everything up in about 20 minutes, including the direct deposits.

4. **Life Insurance.** Life insurance isn't for everyone. In fact, if you don't yet have any dependents, it might not be necessary unless you want to surprise mom and dad with a cash gift upon your demise. The purpose of life insurance is to replace your income in the event of your death and potentially to cover some funeral costs as well.

There are two types of life insurance: term and full. Term life insurance means that you are covered for a certain number of years, for example 10 or 20. If you die after that period, you get nothing. Full life insurance means your family will get a payout even if you die at age 90. It sounds like a no-brainer. After all, why wouldn't you want to get something in return for all of those premiums even if you do make it to be a seriously old fart?

Well, the catch is that a full life policy is much more expensive in terms of the premiums that you pay (think several hundred dollars per month) because essentially it is an investment strategy rather than insurance.

However, if you were going to invest that much money every month, there are more lucrative ways to do it. Plus, if we go back to the original purpose of why we took out the insurance, to replace our income for our family, then it is also worth noting that they may only *need* our full income for the next 20 years or so. By that time your kids might be out of college and earning their own money, your mortgage may be paid off so your spouse may need less money to live off, and so on. For most people term insurance makes much more sense. You can also have two (or more) term policies with different lengths in place to cover the changing financial needs that you anticipate for your family or if you feel as though you need to add more insurance at a later date. For example, you might have one term policy for 30 years to cover your spouse's expenses and another simultaneous one for 20 years that would cover your kids through college. Once you reach retirement age and start living off Social Security and your retirement savings, then your spouse automatically receives your benefits, so a term plan should only go up until the age that you plan to stop working.

The next logical question you may have is how much to insure yourself for. A number that comes close to your annual salary multiplied by the length of the term is a good place to start. However, even if you are a homemaker, you still have a financial value attached to you. Consider how much it would cost to replace the services that you provide to your family. For example, to hire someone to take over child care, cleaning, and cooking. This must of course be tempered by how much money the surviving spouse would save by no longer covering the expenses of the deceased. A homemaker with expensive tastes and no young children might not be worth insuring, whereas a frugal parent of five might, particularly considering the exorbitant cost of full-time daycare.

You can apply for life insurance online. Most require a medical exam but this is free and can be done at your home or place of work. If you are a healthy non-smoker, you will get a preferred rate. If you have health problems that you fear may push up your premiums or make you ineligible, consider policies that do not require a medical exam—though realize they tend to be more expensive. Make sure that you regularly update the beneficiaries of this insurance. If you get divorced, for example, or if a previous beneficiary passes away.

5. **Home or Renters Insurance.** Your home is likely your biggest asset so you must ensure that it is protected. Contents in-

surance, whether you are a homeowner or renter, is also prudent. You may think that you don't have nice stuff, but the cost of replacing everything from your couch to your toothbrush is likely to be prohibitive due to the sheer quantity of goods. It is a good idea to review this insurance every few years as you will invariably have added to your belongings and may well have fancier stuff by then. If you finance your home with a mortgage as most people do, then it is likely that your lender will require you to have at least basic home insurance. This is because until the loan is paid off the institution is a part owner of the house and it is therefore in their interest to ensure that its value is protected in the event of a disaster such as a fire or flood.

6. **Disability Insurance, Long-Term Care Insurance, and Umbrella Insurance.** Full disclosure, I have none of these. Whether or not you need them is dependent on your circumstances. At my age (29 and 96 months), I am far more likely to become disabled than die, however the cost of disability insurance felt prohibitive to me as a self-employed person, considering I have various income streams and could still work on most of them

if I were anything less than severely disabled. This is clearly not the case if you are a ballet dancer, horse trainer, or work in any other field that requires an element of physicality. Long-term care insurance tends to be taken out by people who are a little older than me, say 29 and 372 months (or 60 years old if we are being blunt). This insurance covers a host of services that aren't covered by your health insurance policy, including assistance with daily tasks such as dressing, bathing, or eating. As well as covering services received in your home, this insurance usually covers care received in a senior living center, assisted living facility, or adult daycare.

Umbrella insurance covers events that aren't covered by your home, business, auto, or life insurance; for example, if someone sues you. All of these insurance types may be a great fit for you, so you should speak with an expert before deciding whether or not to take a policy out.

7. **An Estate Plan and Guardianship.** Everyone should have an estate plan, as one thing is certain, we are all going to die someday. This plan covers what is going to happen to all of your stuff, and seeing

as your "stuff" includes any children you might have, parents ought to make this a priority. Finding an estate lawyer and having them set up a plan for temporary and permanent guardianship is key if you want to keep your children out of the foster care system for even a brief period while things are worked out.

My plan lists three "temporary guardians" who live within 20 minutes of my house. They all have a letter authorizing them to take my children with immediate effect should something happen to me. Without this, the police would have to bring them into the station while the permanent guardians (who live much further away) made arrangements to pick them up. Once it is time for the permanent guardians to take over, I have three listed in order of preference. It's not really a popularity contest; the first ones on the list are the ones whom I believe would find it the least inconvenient to take on my kiddos. Luckily they are also the ones who know them best.

In addition to guardianship, I had my lawyer set up a trust into which I have placed most of my assets. This will make them much more simple to pass on as they will avoid the probate system. I have made my permanent guardians trustees of this (as well as beneficiaries of my life insurance) so that they can access the funds that they need to keep my children in iPads and plastic princess shoes.

A will is the final piece of this puzzle if you want to leave items or money to specific people. You can draw up a simple one online or have your estate attorney take care of it as part of his or her package. I would recommend the latter if you can afford it as the wording in wills is extremely important and can make all of the difference when it comes to whether your wishes can be carried out or not. You are going to want to revisit all of this from time to time if your assets change, your guardians move, or you become estranged or divorced from anyone. This step offers rich rewards in terms of peace of mind, though. Knowing that I have set up my family for the least amount of stress should I meet my maker prematurely makes me feel like a great mom even when kids are acting like savages in Trader Joe's and I am pretending that I don't know them.

As you get each item in place, I would like you to start a simple but very important habit. Put a copy of your proof of insurance or new account information in the folder that you purchased at the beginning of the book. Then, every time you get a new bank statement or quarterly statement from your retirement or investment accounts, I would like you to file it in the same folder.

Throw away the old statements for simplicity, because if you end up needing those at a later date they are easy to print out online.

You now have a folder with an up-to-date financial snapshot ready to go. If you meet with a financial advisor you can just grab it, and there at your fingertips will be the answer to any questions he may have.

Let your spouse or a trusted friend know where you keep this folder. That way, should anything happen to you, all of your assets and your life insurance will be organized and at the fingertips of those who need them.

ACTION STEPS

1. Work on getting all of the above items in place.

2. If you can't afford to stock an emergency fund just yet, you can still open the account and set up a direct deposit of $10 per month. This will mean that all of the hard work has been taken care of and all you need to do in the future is increase the amount that you contribute every month.

3. Shop around for life insurance online if you need it and set up an appointment through the insurance company for your physical.

4. Work on your estate plan, especially if you have children.

5. If you are unable to complete these tasks, schedule some time in your calendar to go back to them. Continue to do this until you have the entire list checked off.

6. Start filing your most recent statements in your folder and let a trusted friend or family member know where you keep it

CHAPTER SUMMARY

- Setting up the items above will ensure that you are financially prepared for almost anything.

- Most Americans do not have all of these items in place.

- Even if you don't have the ability to fund all of the accounts now, setting them up gets most of the hard work out of the way.

- Keep a copy of all these documents in your folder. This makes them easy to grab for a meeting with a financial advisor and easy for your family to find should something awful happen to you.

CHAPTER 10
CHOOSING AND
MEETING WITH
A FINANCIAL
ADVISOR
(WITHOUT
TINDER)

"**Y**ou know, I tell my clients that choosing a financial advisor is a bit like going on a first date," Alex once told me.

"Why? Because you might get roofied and then left for dead in an alley?" I asked.

"Er...no, because you need to be compatible. Gosh, dating is so different for women."

Avoid the negative influence of your own instincts by outsourcing your investing to a professional money manager.

As we discussed earlier in the book, our brains make it very plain to us that they don't want to think about money, so it makes perfect sense to outsource that burden to a financial advisor, whose job it is to simplify complex information and take the reins when it comes to investing. Plus, if you want to get better at something, you should always hire a coach, and nowhere is this more important than when it comes to managing our money on a day-to-day basis.

What is interesting about this industry is that financial advisors and finance experts in general are no less prone to falling for the prejudices and mind tricks that we have discussed in this book. They are, in fact, humans just like the rest of us. Plus, financial advice is a lot like dating advice in that it is much easier to *give* objective advice on the subject than to *follow* our own advice. This is why many financial advisors have their own advisors watching over their money to act as a shield against their own instincts.

If you are still in the early stages of your financial journey and have little to invest, then it may not be worth most traditional advisors' time to sit down and work on a detailed financial plan for you as most earn fees based on a percentage of your investable assets. In this case you may want to entail the help of a fee-based advisor who charges, say, by the hour to to get you and keep you on the right track. You could combine this with a robo-advisor and this will help you not just to build up your assets but give you some real-world experience in how investing works.

Once you have some assets built up and are engaged in a regular savings strategy, it is time to shop around for a more permanent solution. A good advisor will take a holistic view of your life and circumstances and tailor a portfolio and financial plan that perfectly suits your needs. From there they will keep you on the right path, offering guidance and reassurance and saving you from yourself when psychological triggers make you want to act against your own best interests.

Compatibility is key when it comes to a successful relationship with your advisor.

The first thing to look for is, Alex says, is someone whom you are compatible with. One of the main predictors of success in a client/therapist relationship is Therapeutic Alliance. This is the relationship and bond created between the provider and the person receiving the therapy, basically whether or not you *like* them. The relationship between a financial advisor and a client is similar. The main predictor of whether or not you will achieve the desired behavioral changes around money is whether or not you like the person whom you are going to be taking advice from. After all, we humans have been frustrating financial advisors for years. We don't act rationally and we tend to dislike their advice in spite of the fact that we ask (and pay!) them for it. A successful advisor might conclude that their role is not merely educating clients or choosing their investments but often simply holding their hands as they persuade them to make decisions that, although correct in an economic sense, go against their most basic instincts.

Screen your advisor thoroughly.

Secondly, you want to make sure that you are going to be working with someone who is honest and upfront. A good way to predict this is how they answer the question of how they get paid. If their answer makes you feel at all uncomfortable then walk away. This is a simple question and it demands a simple answer.

Thirdly, you should ask them what their investment strategy is. They should be able to answer this in a couple of minutes in a way that you can understand. If they start using a lot of industry jargon, promise large returns or very little risk, walk away. Nothing can be guaranteed when it comes to financial markets.

Once you have satisfied yourself with these preliminary investigations, it's time to stalk them online. Pretend you are about to go on a date with them. Wouldn't you want to know if they had a criminal record? Had been investigated for fraud? Thankfully because of the gravity of their profession and the trust that we consumers are required to put in them, there is an organization that provides a public database for screening potential financial advisors called FINRA (Financial Industry Regulatory Board). It is an easy way to uncover any obvious red flags. You may also be able to find them on Yelp! or another review site, although not all advisors choose to have much of a web presence, and those who work for a firm may not be allowed to do it.

Meet with several advisors before you commit.

Ideally you should interview several advisors to ensure you have found the right fit, which is the same advice that I would give anyone joining Tinder. After all, you will need to be comfortable enough with them to share your most personal information: a cancer diagnosis, if you are considering a divorce, thinking of having children, or are experiencing a change in your job situation.

The golden rule is that at the first meeting, they should be asking all about you. If they are truly planning to create a personalized plan for your finances then they need to know about your background, family, risk tolerance, and current financial situation. Alex says that at his initial meetings with clients he tries to maintain a ratio where the client is doing 90% of the talking and he is doing 10%.

Reduce your stress levels by meeting outside of the office if this is a possibility.

Meeting with an advisor for the first time can be daunting, but tests have shown that you can reduce stress levels by doing this in a less formal setting. Find out if your advisor is willing to meet in a café instead of their office. Secondly, bring the folder we discussed in the last chapter. If you are anything like me, being put on the spot over your finances can feel very uncomfortable, so having all of your information with you can be a real confidence booster. If you are asked a question that stumps you, you can simply pull out the statement for the account in question and have them look over it.

ACTION STEPS

1. Research a few good candidates to interview.

2. Ask family and friends who their financial advisor is or run an online search.

3. Interview multiple advisors and choose the one who feels like the best fit.

4. Bring your folder with you so you have access to any information they might need.

Chapter Summary

- Compatibility is a key component to a successful relationship with your financial advisor.

- Decide whether you would benefit most from a traditional advisor, a fee-based advisor, or a financial coach.

- If you aren't ready to work with a financial advisor, start investing using a platform such as Betterment.

- Do your due diligence and look up your advisor on the FINRA website.

- Interview several candidates and ask them how they get paid and what their strategy is.

- Make sure that they let you do most of the talking.

- Bring your folder with you.

CHAPTER 11
HOW TO CUT
YOUR SPENDING
WITHOUT
RUINING
YOUR LIFE

I put this chapter toward the end of the book simply because I feel that when most of us make a decision to "be more responsible with money," cutting spending is the first step that we take. Yet without the proper infrastructure set up for managing our money, the change tends only to be temporary. After all, cutting your spending isn't very appealing if you can't immediately funnel that cash into a specific goal. This is why I wanted to first have you to set up a structure for your finances, so that any savings that you make start flowing in the right direction even if it is at this point just a trickle. As you save or earn more money, that trickle will become a stream and then a river, but it will always flow naturally along the right path as it has already been worn into the rock.

Why do you overspend in the first place?

The truth is that many of us are over-spenders and like any compulsive behavior, the reasons lie deep in our psyche. Marsha Richens and Myron Watkins, marketing professors at the University of Missouri, sought to discover why in their study "Materialism, Transformation Expectations, and Spending: Implications for Credit Use." Their finding was that people with overspending and debt problems tend to share one common trait and that is an overblown expectation of how material goods will make their life better.

The study identified four typical misconceptions that are common to over-spenders.

1. People will like me more
2. I will become a better person
3. I will become more fun
4. I will become more effective

Let's explore these one at a time. Firstly, the idea that people will like you more if you buy certain items. It sounds silly to say out loud, but the truth is that it is an easy trap to fall into because of the way that we humans project ourselves when it comes to viewing other people's spending. What I mean by this is that when we see some guy in a Ferrari, our thoughts tend to be, "Wow, I would look cool and sexy in that car!" This leads us to thoughts of being more desirable, loved, and admired by others. But we rarely think, "Wow, *that guy* looks cool and sexy in that car!" and then feel desire, love, or admiration for *him*. In fact we barely think of him at all beyond the fact that we ourselves would look awesome in his car.

A Ferrari will do no more or less than that for you. You can't trigger feelings such as admiration, desire, and love with material goods; they are triggered by who you are as a person. If you are someone who catches yourself spending to impress others, then pause for a moment to think about the favorite people in your life. Do you love them because they have a beautiful house or car? Or do you love them for their kindness and their willing to be there for you in hard times?

When you next catch yourself on the verge of an extravagant purchase, pause for a moment and ask yourself if you are about to use your money in a way that you think will control others' feelings, or in a way that will positively affect your own. Go back to the Financial Values that you wrote down and see if that purchase fits in with them.

Spending won't make you a better person, but spending in a way that aligns with your personality may make you happier.

Next there is the idea that spending can make you a better person. In a study that was published in *Psychological Science* in April, scientists discovered that people are happiest when their spending is in line with their personalities. Outgoing people, for example, are happy when they spend their spare cash at the pub, while introverts are happy when they spend on books. If you are someone who takes true pleasure spending in ways that make you feel more in touch with your own positive attributes, then focus on those and try to cut spending in other areas. If you want to take it one step further, then try reducing your spending even in the areas that *do* make you feel like a better person. If you love books then start going to the library or sign up for Kindle Unlimited to keep the costs down. If you are a socialite then organize a hiking trip, picnic, or other thrifty activities with friends.

If you think spending money will make you more fun, then you need to get more creative. Whether you are fun to be around or not depends on your personality and your ability to maintain a positive attitude during activities. Advertisers love to show us "fun dad" mountain biking with the kids or "fun girl at the bar" with a glass of champagne raised at the ready. The truth is "fun dads" do silly voices when reading with their children, make couch forts, and set up Easter Egg hunts. Buying a set of mountain bikes for the family might make for a fun outing, but it doesn't make you a fun person. Equally, "fun girl" would be just as fun waving a Miller Lite in the air...or a glass of orange juice for that matter. If you happen to prefer champagne then of course that's another story.

Television persuades us that our spending defines us.

If you want to stop making purchases that you think will change who you are, then switch off the TV. It's not just commercials; even the television shows with their product placements and inaccurate depictions of "real life" can easily convince us that our lives would be improved with more stuff. If you are serious about saving then a short-term boost to your wallet can often be had simply by giving yourself a vacation from all of that propaganda. Head to the library, grab some self-improvement books that focus on the areas that you want to improve on, and dedicate a couple of weeks to doing the inner work that you have been trying to buy your way out of.

Spending might make you more effective, but it isn't the most effective way to achieve this.

The idea that spending can make a person more effective is another concept that your brain likes to present you with when seeking the rush of an impulse purchase. This one is slightly more complex as it can sometimes be true. If you want to become a better writer, then purchasing an instructional book on the topic might well help you. As might a course, coaching program, or a faster laptop.

However, the most efficient ways to improve your productivity come without a price tag: consistency, repetition, progress tracking, and accountability, to name a few. These aren't as sexy to your brain, however, as they offer no initial buyer's rush and the benefits can only be seen over time rather than immediately. Before you buy anything to improve your effectiveness, ask yourself if this is genuinely the best way to achieve your goal or if your brain is merely providing you with a shortcut to the *feeling* of being more effective without actually increasing your productivity.

Cut spending on the least painful areas first and hang on to the luxuries that are most important to you.

Now that we have examined the justifications that our brain presents us with for overspending, it is time to look for some areas that we can cut back on. The internet is full of websites and influencers who go into great detail on this topic so

I won't delve too deeply. I am just going to show you a few places where you may find low-hanging fruit in terms of cutting back. In order to make the changes as painless as possible, I like to focus on ways that I can cut my spending, not my lifestyle. This means making every dollar count.

For example, I am happy to buy the off-brand of everything in the grocery store (particularly the high-end ones such as Whole Foods and Trader Joe's). I almost never buy clothes that aren't on sale, and my car was born three years before my 12-year-old; however, my bath soap costs $24 per bar. I am well aware that I could go to the dollar store and get a pack of Irish Spring for 1/24th of the cost, but every night I lie in my bath and luxuriate in the smell of my Jo Malone soap. It makes me feel fancy and sexy and it lasts for about 60 days, so it's only 40 cents a go. There are worse vices to have than that one, so I see no reason to downgrade. If you aren't the type of person who is beguiled by a posh bath, then this would be a total waste of money. Be your own Marie Kondo when you examine your spending and ask yourself, does this purchase spark joy? If not, nix it.

Look for uncontrolled leaks in your finances.

The most painless step you can take toward improving your finances is to stem any blood flow. Seriously, bolt across the room, rip your belt out of your pants, and apply a very tight tourniquet to your money. You could yell "HELP!" for added drama, and in fact if you have people around you who are contributing to your debt or could be a good source of support, it is a great idea to get them involved. If they don't grasp the severity of the situation, then grab them by the collar and cry "Our money is dying," with a stricken look on your face. It really is, though. Money is like a pot plant; if it isn't actively growing you will have an empty spot on your window ledge before too long.

Blood flow in my opinion is any money that is leaking unintentionally and unnecessarily out of your bank account every month. So let's pull your latest bank or credit card statement from your folder and take a long, hard look at it. Are there any recurring charges on there that could be removed? A gym membership that you no longer use, for example? I once signed up for a relatively reasonably priced gym but never ended up going because...well, I just don't like going to the gym. After six months I felt guilty enough to go in for a short swim and a long shower. Four months after that I watched a little TV on a treadmill. Due to the infrequency of my visits, each one ended up costing $300 and I still had cellulite.

Now I regularly frequent a much more expensive joint to take barre classes. It costs $130 per month but there are free margaritas on Fridays and I make sure to drink around $30 worth. Realistically, this means it only costs me $10 per month. It sparks much more joy, is much cheaper per session as I go so regularly, and I can't see my cellulite at least once a week because I am drunk. It isn't a great example of cutting costs, as on paper I now spend more than twice as much on fitness, but in my defense this has now become spending that benefits me, rather than a pointless outflow if cash.

If you do have a gym membership that you can't afford, then consider trading it in for a pair of sneakers and take up jogging followed by some pull-ups on the playground equipment at the local park. If you are someone who needs motivation to work out, then check out Meetup.com for fit friends or join the Hash House Harriers, the self-professed Drinking Club with a Running Problem. You probably shouldn't booze every time you run, but you might meet a good running partner or two there for the other days, and it's free.

Once you have checked your bank account for weird direct debits that can be axed, then see if you can reduce those that can't be erased completely. Sometimes all it takes is threatening to change phone or internet providers to get a better deal. If they won't budge then try calling competitors and allowing them to seduce you with a deep and dirty discount for switching over. Alternatively, ask a parent or friend if they can add a line to their plan and you can pay them back. It's usually much cheaper than a standalone plan.

If you have cable, then switch to Netflix, Hulu, or one of the newer on-demand services. Find (or make!) a friend who still has cable and go to their house with a bottle of wine to watch the big-ticket shows and games.

Focus on big ticket, easy savings.

If you type "savings tips" into Google you will be inundated with suggestions from extreme couponing, to growing your own produce, to line drying clothes and brewing your own beer. You can't do all of these, nor would that be sensible. You must learn to pick and choose where the greatest rewards lie. This depends both on your financial circumstances and your free time.

If you are a stay-at-home mom on a very tight budget with kids in school or are unemployed then sure, clip coupons. If not then the time spent saving 20 cents on toilet paper is probably not worth it and you should focus on areas where larger savings may be made, such as Groupon or Living Social.

I discussed putting a value on your time in Chapter 4 and this is another area in which to do this. Calculate the value of any savings that you are going to make over the time needed to achieve them. Strategies that can be automated should be given high priority. For example I use two apps when I shop online. The first is Wikibuy, which I run as a browser extension. It tracks prices online, and when I look up products a pop-up shows me the cheapest place to buy that product, automatically tries coupon codes, and in some instances offers me cash back. Every Christmas I log into the account and I usually find around $100 in cash back, which can be converted into a gift card. The other one that I use is Paribus. I don't get huge savings here but as it is automated, anything counts. They track my Amazon deliveries and for each one that is late they send me a message to copy and paste into Amazon's customer service chat window, asking for a refund on shipping or a portion of my Prime membership.

Know exactly where your financial black holes are.

Once you have exhausted these options and stemmed the initial blood flow, then take a look at where exactly your money is going. Knowledge is power and cash is a slippery little sucker. Sometimes it can escape even right under your nose. A quick sandwich here, a few appetizers there, and somehow $700 is shimmying out of your account every month. Mint.com offers a free app that allows you to connect all of your bank and credit card accounts so that you can see exactly where your money is going. There is a little setup involved and I think it only truly comes into its own after a few months of use, when you have had time to categorize everything and create reasonable budgets. Still, looking at your spending in black and white for the first time is a sobering and hopefully motivating experience. YNAB (You Need a Budget) is another popular app for budget tracking on your phone.

After concluding that you are never eating out again, place your hands over your eyes, splay your fingers, and take a tiny peek at the bigger picture. Can you afford your current lifestyle? Do you have more money coming into your account than leaving it? If not it's time to make some big changes. It is likely that your biggest expenditure is housing. They say the cost of your accommodation should be no more than 30% of your gross monthly income. This is, however, a huge generalization and doesn't take into account your personal circumstances. If you have pressing debts and no retirement savings, you need to pay less for your housing, no matter what portion of the pie it currently consumes. Does this mean you need to sell up and move to the neighborhood with bars on the windows? Not necessarily. And if your financial hardship is likely temporary rather than permanent, then the costs of selling a property or moving might outweigh the benefits. Could you perhaps instead take in a housemate?

When I was in college I lived in a shared house with three other girls. One of the girls and I decided to economize even further by sharing a room. I moved onto her floor and we moved another student into my old room. We used the extra cash to pay off our student loans faster. Just kidding. We actually blew it all on clothes like a pair of idiots, but you get the idea: an empty room equals money. Could you get a roommate? Rent it out on Airbnb? Or if you can't stomach any additional human interaction, could you offer it up as storage space for a monthly fee?

Convert clutter to cash.

Now take a look around your house. See all of that clutter? It used to be money. See if you can transform it back into its former glory. If you bought any high-value items or appliances in the last 90 days, then see if you can return them and get a cheap replacement from Craigslist instead. I am not saying that you can never have a matching washer and dryer or a drive-in movie theater-sized TV. I am just saying that if you are looking for some quick cash to pay down debt or stock your emergency fund, then this might be it. Sell unwanted items on online marketplaces or host a yard sale with your neighbors. Try to be organized when you use auction sites and list a large number of items on the same day. That way you should only have to make one trip to the post office when they sell.

See if you can save on food.

This is by far my biggest expenditure after housing, and I am constantly working to reduce it. Our
parents love to tell us that their generation didn't
get to where they are financially by blowing every
bit of spare change on acai bowls and $5 lattes, but
it was easier for them to be thrifty as they lived
in a dark age before such luxuries were invented.
For them breakfast was a bowl of lukewarm, clot-
ted oatmeal and a cup of Folger's coffee. The cost
of such a meal even in today's pricing is just a few
cents versus about $14 for the aforementioned
"superfoods" at the local coffee shop.

However, if you are not ready to downgrade all
the way to prison rations, there are ways to
enjoy an Instagramable breakfast in your own
home. You can bulk-buy frozen acai at Costco,
and a dozen pasture-raised, privately educated
eggs cost about $7. Toss in an avocado (free if
you live in California and your neighbor's tree
is close enough—yay me!) and a secondhand es-
presso machine from eBay and you can breakfast
like a clean-eating queen for two or three dollars
per day. On weekends take turns to host rather
than attend brunch and make it a potluck. Those
"bottomless" mimosas made with cheap champagne and concentrated orange juice will cost you
about $3 per person rather than $20 and as you
will already be in your house you can really get

your money's worth without risking a DUI.

Lunch and dinner provide even more ways to save. If you are buying lunch from a deli every day, then you need to squash that right now, Paris Hilton. It takes a little more work but the savings add up really fast on this one. Even if you buy the fancy bagged salad with the squeezy pack of poppyseed dressing and cranberry nut crunch topping (yum), it will work out at about $1 a portion, and you can toss half a chicken breast or some shrimp on top for just a couple dollars more. Or go full fourth grade and treat yourself to a PB&J and a cheese string. Add an inspiring quote to read back to yourself as you chow down, such as
"A PB&J today is better than cat food when I am 80," to keep you motivated.

We live in California with a huge pack of children so our grocery bill is appalling. I'm talking $1-2k per month which would make my European friends (whose grocery prices benefit from farm subsidies) faint. After years of wrestling with my food budget, I have employed the following methods that work for me:

1. **I shop my pantry first when meal-planning.** For some bizarre reason, it always feels like more effort to me to dig around the back of my pantry than it does to put on pants, drive to the store, and buy something new. I have had to be very strict with myself to instill this habit.

2. **I shop for the lowest prices on staples and then I buy them in bulk.** I use the Basket App to do this. It allows me to search a single product, such as chicken breasts, and then it will give me the pricing for these in all of the local grocery stores. If there is a particularly good deal, I purchase the whole shelf and freeze what I don't need that week. We also do a big monthly shop at Costco and I use their coupon book for that. If they have anything non-perishable that we regularly use on sale then I buy the maximum amount allowed and store it in the garage. Think dishwasher tabs, toilet paper, or long-lasting foods such as peanut butter, tuna, and crackers.

3. **I order groceries online.** While grocery delivery is expensive, having someone pick items off the shelf for you is usually very cheap or free. As well as saving me an entire hour, it means I impulse purchase less. I have also discovered that most stores will automatically apply coupons for you (no clipping!) so I feel as though I save more than I spend even if there is a fee associated with the service.

4. **I try to meal plan.** This is a habit that often falls by the wayside because with five children all enrolled in different activities, our schedule is far from regular. However, when I am on my A game I use the Cozi app to save recipes, make shopping lists, and plan meals for the week. It is easy to use and you can share access with your partner.

Go vegetarian...sometimes!

When it comes to dinner, we can easily find ourselves in the habit of the meat and two veg model. This is an expensive way to eat particularly if like me you can't stomach factory-farmed meat and find yourself handing over a small fortune for bacon that grew up in the Hamptons instead of a gestation crate. One way to save is by purchasing cheaper cuts and slow-cooking them. This makes for some seriously delicious meals if you have the time. If you don't, there is the Instant Pot (or another brand of pressure cooker). This will turn a chewy old chuck roast into melt-in-your-mouth stew in under an hour.

If you want to save even more, go vegetarian for a few meals a week. Look abroad for delicious recipes featuring pulses that offer protein and fiber for a planet- and gut-saving punch. Millennials are being affected by staggeringly high rates of colon cancer at the moment from a veg-light diet, so a creamy Indian lentil curry or some Venezuelan rice and beans will make you a winner on all fronts.

Can't cook? There's a YouTube tutorial for that.

If you aren't an accomplished chef, don't panic. YouTube is full of simple instructional videos that you can cook along with thanks to your smartphone. Find a chef you can relate to. Some of them are super-hot. Some of them cook with no shirt on. Some of them actually make good food. I don't know your priorities here, but I am just trying to get across the point that there is a YouTube cooking channel out there for you whatever your dietary preference and tolerance for watching someone's bare skin hovering dangerously close to a pan full of hot oil. Sometimes I have to watch through my fingers.

Become a cheap date.

One area of life that should never be neglected no matter how dire your finances is your love life. No matter whether you are single, married, or in some kind of weird poly-amorous sect, it is important to invest in your romantic relationships.

Alex and I try to maintain a weekly "date night," and depending on the state of our finances it might look like a fancy dinner followed by a trip to the theater or it might simply involve banishing our children upstairs and enjoying a quiet(er) dinner together on the patio.

One of the biggest expenses of dating, or indeed socializing in any capacity, as a parent is the babysitter. See if you can find local parents who want to swap babysitting duties with you or host your children for sleepovers if you return the favor the following week. I also like to tell friends and relatives that if they are shopping for me for Christmas or my birthday, I am a size BABYSITTER. By committing to spending an evening with my delightful kiddos, they are gifting me a service that would cost me about $80 at no cost to them. It is a win-win for everyone!

If we have scored a free or paid babysitter but have little in the way of extra funds for a night out, then we love packing a simple picnic and enjoying it anywhere that isn't our house. If you are newly dating or have no kids, this is still a great, thrifty, and very romantic option. But stay safe out there, people, and avoid going to, say, a heavily wooded area with someone unless you know that person extremely well. Explain to your Tinder date that you would love to share a picnic with them but it has to be on the floor of the Westfield Mall on a Saturday.

ACTION STEPS

1. Set up your financial infrastructure before you cut your spending.

2. Take a TV detox if you find you are spending to change others' perceptions of you. Identify your real issues and work on them in that time.

3. Cut spending in the least painful areas. Stop any financial leaks and identify which luxuries are worth keeping to you.

4. Download a budgeting app to get clarity on your spending and to identify black holes.

5. Check your spending for value. For example, a gym that costs $130 per month that you visit four to five times a week is a better deal than one you pay $50 to but never visit.

6. Start meal planning, eat less meat, and learn to cook at home using YouTube if needed.

7. Become a cheap date and start a babysitting trade.

Chapter Summary

- Set up your financial infrastructure before you start saving. There is no point cutting spending if that money has nowhere useful to go.

- The four misconceptions that are common to overspenders are:

     1. People will like me more
     2. I will become a better person
     3. I will become more fun
     4. I will become more effective

- Spending in line with your personality will make you happier so be sure to use your money mindfully.

- Television brainwashes us into thinking our spending can change who we are, but this is entirely false.

- Cut spending in the least painful areas first and stop any financial leaks.

- Examine the value of the things that you do spend money on. Are they useful? Do they spark joy?

- Save money on food by meal planning and cooking at home. You don't always need to base your meals around expensive meat.

- Become a cheap date and see if you can set up a babysitting trade if you have kids.

CHAPTER 12
HOW TO FEEL INCREDIBLY SMUG BECAUSE YOU'VE DONE IT!

After doing all of this research, I am painfully aware that making complex and emotionally charged decisions about your finances will not have scored highly on the list of things you have enjoyed this year. However, you may find that the systems that you have put into place, the habits you've formed, the provisions you have made for your family, and the savings you have started to amass will mean that the work that you have just done will eventually change your life in ways that our linear-thinking brains can barely process.

Let almighty automation be your salvation!

The key to your success now is to simply maintain your well-oiled financial machine. Take a moment to go back over all of the Action Steps that we talked about and make sure you have automated them all as much as possible. Your savings and retirement accounts should be growing without you lifting a finger as direct deposits whizz back and forth between your accounts. Your bills should be drawing directly from your account at the beginning of your pay cycle, and your assets and children should be protected with insurance and a solid estate plan. All of the information that you or anyone else might need to get a snapshot of your current financial picture should be readily available and organized in your folder.

We talked about the emotional effect that money has on humans due to our hairy caveman brains and how when it comes to financial decisions, high-powered investment bankers fall prey to their own gut reactions as easily as the rest of us. Money, like love, isn't science. It involves a lot of heavy breathing and sweaty palms, but when we respond to our financial circumstances with gut feelings as opposed to rational thought, we tend to make terrible decisions. This means that finding a great financial advisor, coach, or trusted buddy to provide emotionally disconnected, impartial advice is invaluable, particularly as you start investing in a more serious manner.

Keep a cool head around your investments.

If we want to enjoy the success of our fabulous old couple, Earl and Martha, then we need to continue to work on becoming exponential thinkers when it comes to our wealth. Part of this involves investing in and riding out the bumpy parts of the stock market. Be an optimist! Newspapers declaring that the world is in dire straits sell more than those reassuring us that everything is ticking along nicely. In financial terms indulging in this type of pessimism leads us to fall back on our linear thinking. If we put our $20k savings into a CD making 2% we are guaranteed steady if not very exciting growth. In fact, it would take 35 years to double our money to $40k. If that $20k were invested in a manner that averaged an annual growth of 7% then the money would be doubled in just 10 years.

The upside for linear thinkers is that it allows them to avoid any risk, which they convince themselves will wipe them. But in today's world we have every reason to be optimistic and should act accordingly, indulging in our pessimism only to ensure that we leave enough of a margin in our calculations for bumps in the ride. This might mean ensuring that the timeframe for liquidating our $20k investment is somewhat flexible and that we balance our investments so that our risk is aligned with our current situation. For example, a 30-year-old can comfortably afford a lot of risk in their retirement portfolio as the money won't be needed for many years, whereas a 60-year-old will need to ratchet back that risk on the basis that they will need access to those funds in a relatively short time.

Keep more of what you earn and make more from what you keep.

Remember that in terms of creating a great long-term strategy for your finances, it is not what you *earn* but what you *keep* that is important. Saving and investing are for everyone, not just rich people. If you have great financial habits, even a relatively small income can go a long way. Keep perfecting your habits a little at a time. *Atomic Habits* by James Clear and *The Power of Habit* by Charles Duhigg are wonderful books to keep you inspired. Make a commitment to yourself to check in on your progress every now and again and schedule it in your calendar so you don't forget.

Surround yourself with inspiring people. If you can't hang out with Warren Buffet or Dave Ramsey in person you can still follow them on Twitter. You are a financial wizard now; these people are your tribe!

Finally, keep learning. Listen to the occasional financial podcast in the car (I like Good Financial

Cents with Jeff Rose), read a couple of books a year, and follow blog or two. I am much too humble to plug mine here, which is located at www.ThisisYourBrainonMoney.com (cough).

However if you are really serious about educating yourself, turbocharging your investing and staying accountable, start sleeping with a financial advisor. It worked for me.

THE END

ABOUT THE AUTHOR

Alice Von Simson

Alice von Simson moved to California in 2007 from London, England. Her first book "Snow White and the Seven Vertically Challenged Citizens" won critical acclaim from her 4th Grade teacher and classmates. After a long break to focus on her passion for underachieving on the beach she has returned with Secrets I Learned by Sleeping with my Financial Advisor, the first book ever to combine online dating and personal finance.

Her website www.ThisisYourBrainonMoney.com aims to bring financial literacy to populations that she considers to be underserved, largely those with short attention spans and better things to do or "my people" as she calls them.

She lives with her financial advisor, his three sons, her daughter, a step daughter from her previous marriage and a baby bump which was a product of the stringent research she did for her latest book.

www.ingramcontent.com/pod-product-compliance
Lightning Source LLC
Chambersburg PA
CBHW071529040426
42452CB00008B/941